Modern world issues

Series editor: John Turner

the arms race

SECOND EDITION

JOHN TURNER

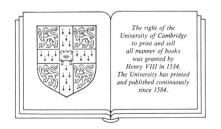

*The right of the
University of Cambridge
to print and sell
all manner of books
was granted by
Henry VIII in 1534.
The University has printed
and published continuously
since 1584.*

Cambridge University Press

Cambridge

New York   New Rochelle

Melbourne   Sydney

For Hazel and Anna

I should like to thank the many organisations and individuals who have helped me in writing this book. SIPRI, World Priorities Inc., CAAT, ADIU and CND have been particularly helpful. Thanks are also due to Jeff McMahan for his helpful suggestions and constructive criticisms, and to staff at CUP, especially to Sally Taylor and Stephanie Boyd for their painstaking work.

Acknowledgements
Illustrations by John Blackman, Tim Watts and Len Huxter

The author and publisher would like to thank the following for permission to reproduce illustrations: front cover Black Star (New York); back cover *The Cobb Book*, © 1975 Ron Cobb, Wild and Woolley, Sydney: opposite p. 1 Pennie Smith; pp. 1, 3, 5, 7 diagrams adapted from *World Military and Social Expenditures* (1979 and 1981) by Ruth Leger Sivard, © World Priorities, Leesburg, VA 22075, USA; p. 8 Bill Mauldin and Wil-Jo Associates Inc.; p. 9 (left) Oxfam; p. 9 (right) New Internationalist Publications Limited; pp. 10, 19, 20 Imperial War Museum; pp. 11, 47 US Department of Defense; pp. 14, 16, 57 (right) US Air Force; p. 17 Stockholm International Peace Research Institute; p. 23 Aerofilms Ltd: p. 24 (left above and below), 39 US Department of Energy; p. 24 (right) Shunkichi Kikuchi and Hiroshima-Nagasaki Publishing Committee; p. 26 *The Salt Lake Tribune*; p. 27 John Hillelson Agency; p. 30 Northrop Corp., California (print from MARS, Lincs.); p. 31 José Lavanderos; p. 34 Syndication International; p. 44 Keystone Press Agency; pp. 44 (left), 71 (below) Tim Watts; p. 44 Ira Wyman/Sygma; p. 57 (left) MOD (RAF); p. 57 (centre left) US Army Photograph; p. 57 (centre right) Boeing Aerospace Company, Seattle (print from MARS, Lincs.); p. 58 The Photosource; p. 59 Duncan Campbell, *War Plan UK*, Burnett Books 1982; p. 60 Bryan McAllister and *The Guardian*; p. 61 Swiss Federal Office of Civil Defence; p. 62 The Washington Post Writers Group; p. 63 the Controller of Her Majesty's Stationery Office; p. 64 Colvic Craft Ltd; p. 70 Sygma; p. 71 (above) Andrew Wiard (Report); p. 72 (left) Lockheed Missiles and Space Company, Lockheed Aircraft Corp./US Navy; p. 72 (right) British Aerospace (print from MARS, Lincs.); p. 78 United Nations; p. 79 Centre for Alternative Industrial and Technological Systems (CAITS). Thanks are due to the Center for Defense Information for their help in collecting photographs from US government departments.

Published by the Press Syndicate of the University of Cambridge
The Pitt Building, Trumpington Street, Cambridge CB2 1RP
32 East 57th Street, New York, NY 10022, USA
10 Stamford Road, Oakleigh, Melbourne 3166, Australia

© Cambridge University Press 1983, 1988

First published 1983
Reprinted 1985
Second edition 1988

Printed in Great Britain at the University Press, Cambridge

Library of Congress cataloging in publication data
Turner, John, 1949 Oct. 17–
  The arms race/John Turner. – 2nd ed.
    (Modern world issues)
  Bibliography: p. 92
  1. Munitions. 2. Arms control. 3. Arms race – History – 20th
  century. I. Title. II. Series.
  UF530.T89   1988
  355.8′2 – dc19   87–13072   CIP

British Library cataloguing in publication data
Turner, John, *1949 Oct. 17-*
The arms race.–2nd ed.–(Modern
world issues).
1. Arms race
I. Title II. Series
355.8′2   U815
ISBN 0 521 34749 1

Contents

The Live Aid rock concert staged simultaneously in London and Philadelphia in July 1985 raised a staggering sum of money – $100 million – to aid starving people in Africa. This reflected the concern and generosity of millions of ordinary people who dipped into their pockets and helped to raise funds to help their fellow human beings. $100 million represents just *one hour*'s worth of world arms spending in 1986. Fourteen thousand African children die each day from hunger-related diseases.

1   What is the arms race?

World spending on arms

What would you do if you had about US $1 700 000 to spend? Such a large amount of money may be hard for you to imagine but perhaps ideas of buying a large house, or a boat, or taking a round-the-world cruise may appeal to you. With that amount of money you could do all these things and still have plenty left over. Possibly you would prefer not to lavish all that money on yourself but would choose to help people who are in greater need than you are, such as those who live in the poorer countries of the world. Indeed, even keeping aside say $400 000 for yourself, the rest could buy at least twenty first-class tractors, as well as other farm equipment, seeds and fertilisers, which would help farmers increase the output from their land and help to feed thousands of people. Alternatively, it could help to build a medical centre in a village so that medical help could be made available to those who have none. Or it could pay for the sinking of wells and the provision of pumps to irrigate parched land. It could be used to build and equip twenty rural schools so that young people could learn to read and write and thus help their country to develop economically. There is an almost endless list of important productive uses for that $1 700 000. You can probably think of many more for yourself.

The amount of money we have just been talking about – $1 700 000 – represents just *one minute's worth* of spending on weapons by the world's nations. Every million or so dollars spent in this way means that those tractors, medical centres, wells and schools may not be built and the people who could have benefited so much from them will have to do without. This book is about the massive investment the world makes in armaments, and the ever rising amounts spent on weapons in what has been known as the 'arms race'.

Never before have so many of the world's resources gone into the production of armaments. In 1986 world spending on armaments reached about $900 billion (R. Sivard, 1986). About twenty per cent of this went on nuclear weapons. Within the next twenty-four hours nearly $2.5 billion will be spent on armaments. In the same twenty-four hours about 40 000 people in the *Third World* will die from hunger and hunger-related diseases. In the same world that spends $1.7 million a minute on weapons, 800 million people (about a fifth of the world's population) live in desperate poverty. The arms race is consuming wealth that could be used to help solve these problems. At a cost of less than half an hour's military spending, the United Nations was recently able to destroy a plague of locusts in Africa. This saved enough grain to feed 1.2 million people for a year.

Valuable human resources go into the arms race. There are about 27 million soldiers world-wide, and a further 50 million people are employed in arms industries in one way or another. The discoveries

Arms spending of the rich nations compared with their aid to the poorest nations, 1960–84

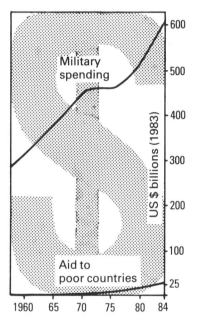

Source for arms spending figures and the graph above: *World Military and Social Expenditures, 1986*

Third World

Although not an entirely satisfactory term, 'Third World' is used in this book to describe the poorer countries of Africa, Asia and Latin America, which are neutral in the East–West alignment.

billion

Note that throughout this book,
'billion' refers to the US billion, i.e.
1 billion = 1 000 000 000

of scientists and the designs of engineers can bring considerable benefits to the world; but well over half a million scientists and engineers are employed in devising and testing new weapons systems.

The world has never spent so much on weapons in peacetime as it does today. The stockpiles of weapons in the world are bigger than ever before. The build-up of weapons is gaining speed and spreading to more and more countries. Each year new weapons are being introduced that are more accurate and deadly than the ones they replace. At the very top of the league of destructive power are nuclear weapons. In 1945 only three such weapons had been built. By 1986 there were about 60 000 of them with a total destructive power 1.25 million times greater than those first bombs. Yet there were plans to add thousands more by the 1990s.

Why is there an arms race?

What has happened? Why has the arms race developed in the way it has? What can be done about it? These are some of the most important questions we shall be tackling in this book. In the first seven chapters we look at the main features of the arms race, and we try to explain why the main countries involved behave as they do. In the final chapter we look at some of the efforts and suggestions that are being made for reversing the arms race. You will not find, at the back of this book, an answer page containing ten easy steps to world peace, but you will find many suggestions about moves that can be taken by groups of ordinary people and by governments to begin to change the direction we are currently taking.

In 1978 the representatives of 149 of the world's governments declared at the United Nations their opposition to the arms race and their desire for disarmament:

> *Removing the threat of a world war – a nuclear war – is the most... urgent task of the present day... Mankind is presented with a choice: we must halt the arms race and proceed to disarmament or face annihilation.*

Despite these fine words, governments have done little since 1978 to slow down, let alone reverse, the arms race. On the contrary, there have been sharp increases both in arms spending and in world tensions in the early 1980s. When it came to translating words into action, most governments seemed to find disarmament unattractive. Why? Political leaders are suspicious of others and are reluctant to reduce armaments in case this should give an advantage to their enemies. Governments may say they are in favour of disarmament without actually meaning it, because there are, as we shall see, powerful groups of people in all of the major countries involved in the arms race who do not want to see a reduction in armaments.

Do the mass of people in the world's nations gain from the arms race? Do they want it? If we believe that the answer to both is, 'no', then the way forward would seem to be to involve far greater numbers of people in decisions about defence and the arms race. In the early 1980s millions of people in several European countries demonstrated against the nuclear arms race. However, it would be foolish to think that, just by demonstrating in the streets, 'the people' alone can halt the arms race. In the first place, not all governments are equally open to influence by the people they represent. Furthermore, there are real causes for mistrust and

Some other ways of spending the money that now goes on armaments ($900 billion per year)

 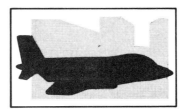 

The money spent on one Chieftan tank ($2.1 million) is equivalent to what it would cost to build 43 homes.

The money spent on one US F-15C fighter ($39 million) is equivalent to what it would cost to build and equip a large general hospital.

The money spent on one Trident nuclear submarine ($1 billion) is equivalent to what it would cost to build several hundred schools.

What could be achieved in the space of a few years if just 10 per cent of what we spend on arms each year went on development projects instead

$2.5 billion	To provide family planning and health care for all mothers
$11 billion	To clean up the world's air and soil and control further pollution
$9.5 billion	To provide clean water for the 2 billion people who do not have it; this would help prevent many diseases such as cholera and hookworm
$4 billion	To provide basic health care for rural areas in the Third World
$7.5 billion	To develop renewable energy sources such as solar energy, water- and wind-power, and to restock forests
$7.5 billion	To provide basic training in work skills for the 50 million young people who start work each year
$4.5 billion	To research and develop low-cost technology that would save on oil and use local resources
$11 billion	To provide schools and teachers for the 50 per cent of children in the Third World who never have the chance of going to school
$10 billion	To provide a long-term food-aid programme which would solve the problems of malnutrition
$4 billion	To teach everyone to read and write
$1.5 billion	To vaccinate all children against diseases such as measles, polio and tetanus which now kill 15 million children a year
$11.5 billion	To help poor farmers by giving better seeds, fertilisers and irrigation. This alone would vastly increase food supplies
$4.5 billion	To save a million lives in Africa alone; by draining swamps and providing medicines to eliminate malaria

Source: The 10 per cent programme, adapted and updated from R. Sivard, *World Military and Social Expenditures, 1979; updated 1986*

---

conflict between the two countries most involved in the arms race, the USA and the Soviet Union. Many governments and people in the West, especially those most closely tied to the USA through the NATO military alliance, believe that the Soviet Union and its allies are intent on dominating the world and on imposing communism upon other nations. Similarly the Soviet leaders and their allies believe that the Western nations are the aggressors who want to dominate the world, destroying the power of the Soviet

Who are the superpowers?

The *superpowers* are countries with massive economic and military resources who therefore take considerable interest in the rest of the world which they try to influence. The two most powerful countries in these respects are the USA and the Soviet Union. China is often regarded as a superpower, but since China is far less militarily powerful and less influential abroad than the other two, it is not included as a superpower in this book.

Union and world communism if possible. These beliefs are encouraged by the fact that the *superpowers* often try to gain power and influence by supplying armaments to friendly governments or to groups that are trying to overthrow the existing government. In this situation, it is difficult for one side to trust the other. Both superpowers regard strong military forces as a kind of insurance policy which has served them both well in the past, and which might be resorted to again if other measures fail. However, in the late 1980s, both the Soviet Union, under Gorbachev, and the USA, under Reagan, seemed more willing to move towards real disarmament. Significant progress was made in talks to reduce the number of nuclear weapons in Europe and elsewhere.

If the arms race is to be halted, several things will have to be done. Of these, two steps are very important. The mass of ordinary people throughout the world must be helped to understand why the arms race has occurred and how it affects their lives. As a result, pressure may increase for governments to take the idea of disarmament more seriously. But little will be achieved unless, at the same time, peaceful solutions can be found to many of the conflicts between nations which lead them to use force; for the arms race is fed by these conflicts. Reductions in the size of armed forces and in levels of weapons could be one direct way of reducing the fears, tension and mistrust that exist between nations, but significant disarmament will only be possible if the underlying causes of conflict are tackled too. Massive public support will be needed if such changes are to be made and if the influence of those who want the arms race to continue is to be reduced. We shall look at possible steps forward in the last chapter, but first it is important to understand the nature of the arms race.

The arms race jigsaw

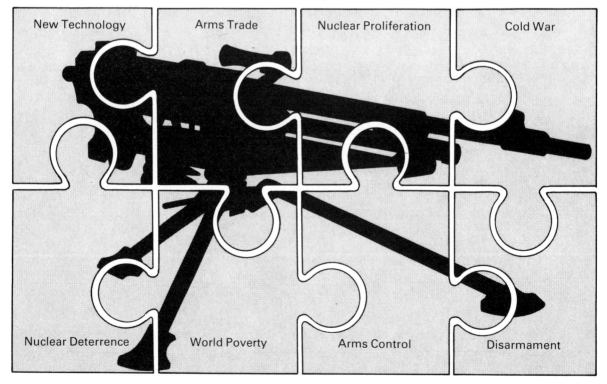

New Technology | Arms Trade | Nuclear Proliferation | Cold War

Nuclear Deterrence | World Poverty | Arms Control | Disarmament

New Technology

What is technology?

Technology is the practical application of scientific and technical discoveries. There have been many important technological developments in the twentieth century in all branches of science. Many of these have been applied to the development of new weapons systems.

Rather like a jigsaw puzzle, the arms race is built out of a number of pieces which lock together to give it an overall shape. How do the pieces fit together?

Part of the rise in world spending on armaments can be accounted for by the increases in the number and variety of weapons that are being manufactured. But of far greater importance are the tremendous improvements that have been made in weapons *technology* since the end of the Second World War. Modern weapons systems can do things which were simply undreamed of only forty-five years ago. The constant effort to improve weapons systems and to devise defences against other people's new weapons has been a major feature of the arms race. This has not only made weapons systems increasingly expensive, but new technology has also revolutionised the way in which wars are conducted and has introduced new and unpredictable dangers into the arms race, particularly where nuclear weapons are concerned.

Arms Trade

World arms exports 1960–83

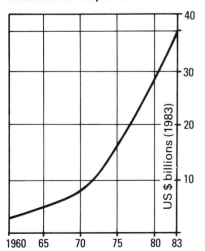

Source: *World Military and Social Expenditures, 1986*

In order to extend their influence, the superpowers have built military alliances with friendly countries to whom they have been increasingly willing to supply the most up-to-date weaponry. Local conflicts and tensions are sometimes fuelled by this *arms trade*, and regional arms races have been encouraged. There is an increased danger that the superpowers, as suppliers of weapons or protectors of friendly governments, may get sucked in to these conflicts. Many of the countries which import large amounts of weapons are very poor. They spend precious money on weapons instead of investing in their economic development. The pattern is particularly common in poor countries which are run by military governments, where the arms may be used against their own people. Although the superpowers continue to be the biggest suppliers, some European and Third World countries have greatly increased their share of the world arms trade in recent years, making the situation less easy to control.

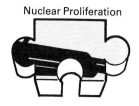

Nuclear Proliferation

A further worry is caused by the *spread of nuclear know-how* to more and more countries. Increasing numbers of countries are building nuclear reactors and so getting nearer to having the ability to make their own nuclear weapons. Although many restrictions have been put upon the use of reactors and upon the possible diversion of nuclear fuel to make bombs, many countries are on the verge of getting nuclear weapons for themselves. Once they do this, the world will become an even more dangerous place.

Cold War

The two main contestants in the arms race are the superpowers. They have the world's biggest military machines, they are the world's biggest spenders, and the biggest producers of weapons for export to the rest of the world. An understanding of the arms race must therefore begin with an understanding of the relationship between the Soviet Union and the USA, especially since 1945 (a more detailed examination of this will be found in Chapter 5). It can be described in terms of mistrust, suspicion and fear. The years since the end of the Second World War have been marked by propaganda battles between the two, and by threats, accusations and sabre-rattling. Occasionally the superpowers have come near to open war – over Berlin in 1948, 1958 and 1961 and over Cuba in 1962. At times of high tension there has been little contact between the Americans and Russians, but when tensions are eased as they were in the early 1970s and late 1980s, it has proved possible for them to co-operate, to seek some controls over armaments and to try to break down the barriers of mistrust and misunderstanding between them.

Nevertheless the tensions that have been termed the *Cold War* have always been present. As a result, both superpowers have built huge military machines which now involve large and powerful groups of people who gain their influence and livelihood from the arms race.

World military expenditures 1960–85

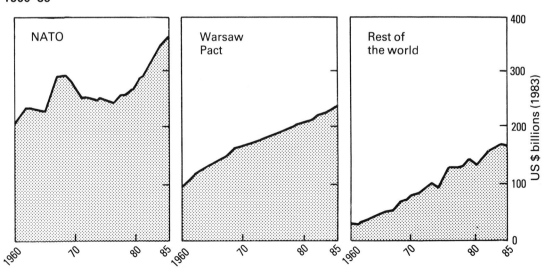

Source: *World Military and Social Expenditures, 1986*

10

NATO and the Warsaw Pact

These two alliances together account for about 75 per cent of the total world spending on armaments. Each alliance is dominated by a superpower: NATO by the USA, the Warsaw Pact by the Soviet Union. France is not a fully integrated member of NATO because her military command is 'independent'.

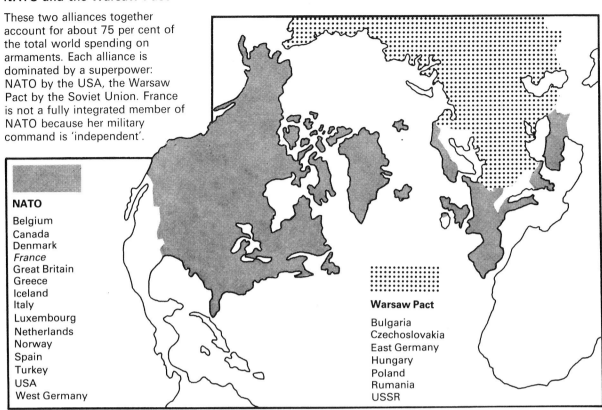

NATO

Belgium
Canada
Denmark
France
Great Britain
Greece
Iceland
Italy
Luxembourg
Netherlands
Norway
Spain
Turkey
USA
West Germany

Warsaw Pact

Bulgaria
Czechoslovakia
East Germany
Hungary
Poland
Rumania
USSR

Different types of weapons

**conventional
nuclear
biological
chemical**

In modern warfare the term *conventional* refers to all weapons which are not *nuclear, biological* or *chemical* weapons. This second group are called *weapons of mass destruction* because they can cause death and injury on such a large scale. *Nuclear* weapons use the radioactive element uranium or plutonium to cause a massive explosion and release of radiation. *Biological* weapons use deadly germs and *chemical* weapons use various kinds of poison in the form of gases or droplets.

Nuclear Deterrence

Both superpowers have built thousands of nuclear weapons of many different kinds and have for many years based their military policies upon the threat of using these weapons against their enemies. This policy is known as *nuclear deterrence*. It is based upon the idea that a country can prevent aggression against it by possessing such powerful weapons that an enemy is too frightened to risk an attack. If deterrence works, then the very threat to use the destructive power of nuclear weapons against an aggressor is enough to stop that aggression and avoid war. Some people argue that the balance of nuclear forces between the two superpowers has prevented war. Others are more worried that the world lives under constant threat of war and the risk that nuclear weapons, if ever used, might destroy the human race altogether. They also argue that many improvements in technology make deterrence increasingly unworkable and war more likely.

"...But we make the world's finest tanks."

World Poverty

What can be done about these problems? An increasing number of people are saying that we cannot go on like this for much longer. The nuclear arms race threatens us all with destruction, while the arms trade worsens the conflicts in the poorer parts of the world and at the same time uses up the valuable resources (money, labour and materials) that could be used to help these countries develop and overcome their problems of *poverty*. The arms race is also a major burden on the world's richer countries. They too have their problems: unemployment, rising rates of crime and the continuing poverty of large sections of their populations. Many people see the arms race as the main obstacle to solving many of the problems facing both the poor and the rich countries of the world. Perhaps it is no coincidence that Japan, with one of the world's strongest and fastest-growing economies, has had the lowest rate of spending on arms of all the industrialised nations.

Arms Control

There is the greatest difficulty in getting countries which have always relied on their military strength to protect them in the past to put any faith in disarmament. However, increasing numbers of people are saying that ways must be found. Many suggestions have been put forward, ranging from limited restrictions on certain types of weapons through to proposals for world-wide general and complete disarmament. The SALT talks between the USA and the Soviet Union which took place in the 1970s are an example of limited *arms control* (see Chapter 8). Another example is the talks that have been going on in Vienna since 1972, trying, without success, to negotiate reductions in conventional forces within Europe. Throughout most of 1987 talks took place in Geneva between the superpowers to reduce two major groups of land-based nuclear missiles. These were genuine disarmament talks.

Disarmament

By the 1980s, however, many people seemed to have lost faith in the ability of the traditional approaches to arms control to stem the arms race. Instead they called for *real reductions* in armaments, either through a negotiated process of stage-by-stage *disarmament*, or by single countries taking the bold step of renouncing their own nuclear weapons as a first step towards full disarmament.

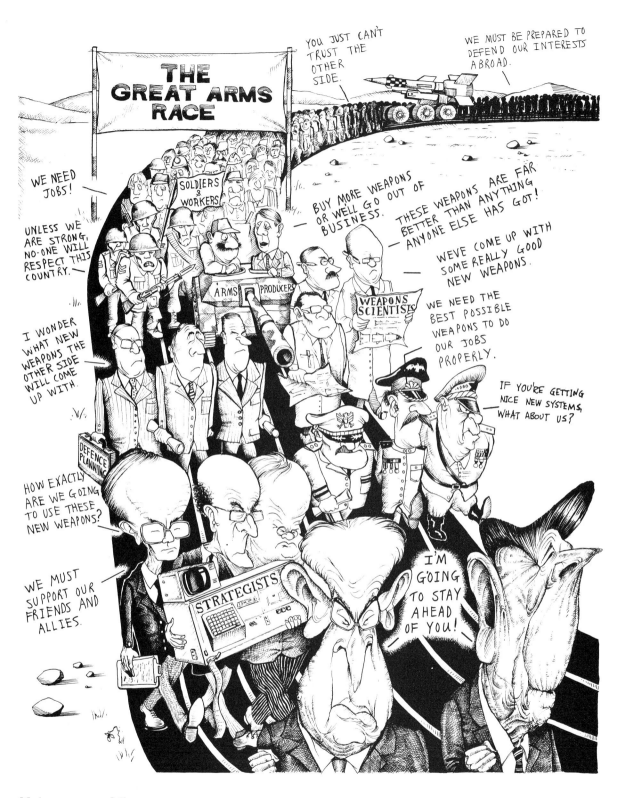

Major causes of the arms race

The arms race is fuelled by many things. International rivalries and conflicts, especially those between the two superpowers, are partly responsible. But in both superpowers there are important domestic pressures and attitudes which tend to drive the arms race onward.

13

2 Modern weapons and warfare

The importance of technology

In this chapter we look at the technology of modern warfare: how the discoveries of scientists and engineers have been applied to modern weapons. Throughout history the inventive power of the human mind has been used to make weapons more deadly. We now have a huge variety of weapons and ways of carrying and controlling them. The rate at which new developments are being introduced is speeding up each year. As we shall see, the latest developments in electronics, particularly micro-computers and miniature circuits, made possible by the use of micro-chip technology, are now being used in the latest generations of weapons. In this chapter we shall see how the technological changes that have taken place in modern weaponry during this century have altered the very nature of modern warfare and have made it possible for people to destroy one another on a huge scale and at a speed never before known to humankind.

Technological developments have been made in weaponry since the very earliest times, but it is only in the twentieth century that such developments have really gathered pace. During the First World War a great deal of effort was put into developing new weapons technology. The use by the Germans of poison gas (first chlorine and later mustard gas) gave them an advantage over other troops until they could be protected by gas masks. At sea the British fleet found itself totally vulnerable for several years because of a small number of underwater boats used by the Germans. By 1918, the 178 Germans U-boats had sunk over 6.5 million tonnes of British merchant shipping. By then, however, several methods of anti-submarine warfare including small attack craft, mines and depth charges had been developed. In 1913 the Wright brothers had made their first flight and within a few years aircraft were being used in the war. Although they were first used to spy on enemy trenches it was soon realised that aircraft could play a more direct role in war fighting. Machine guns were fitted that could be fired through the propellers. Primitive bombs were supplied for pilots to throw

Modern technology has greatly increased the destructiveness of weapons. The scene of devastation (left) was produced by months of shelling, while the entire area (right) was destroyed in only seconds. One picture is of a French battlefield in 1916; the other is of Nagasaki, Japan, in 1945, a few days after an atomic explosion.

overboard. New designs were introduced to enable aircraft to fly faster, carry more weight and climb more steeply. The need to gain advantage over the enemy and to produce inventions that could act in defence against this new technology led to major advances in weapons technology during the First World War.

The same competition was at work during the Second World War and has continued to accelerate ever since. The effort to be ahead in weapons technology has been a very important feature of the arms race, and has never been more important than today when designers and manufacturers are constantly striving to improve the destructiveness of their weapons systems. Much of the mounting cost of the arms race arises from the development and production of new weapons systems. In the past, older weapons systems were sold off or given away to other countries by the most advanced weapons-producing countries. But, increasingly, to help overcome the crippling costs of new weapons, the latest versions are being sold immediately to countries that can afford to pay. Let us look at some of the most important developments in modern weapons systems.

Precision-guided weapons

As the diagram on page 16 shows, there have been major improvements in the design of battle tanks since they were first introduced. But modern tanks now have to face some very effective anti-tank weapons which can sear through the thick armour plating of all but the best-protected tanks. One example is the TOW missile used by NATO forces. Using one missile costing $8400 one soldier can knock out a tank worth $2.1 million up to three kilometres away. The existence of many thousands of these anti-tank missiles means that it is not necessary for one side to match an enemy's number of tanks.

The TOW is just one example of *precision-guided weapons*. The development of guided weapons has dramatically changed the nature of warfare in the last thirty years. The problem with shells, bullets and free-fall bombs is their inaccuracy. In order to destroy a target the explosion must be as near as possible to it. A bullet or shell fired from a gun does not always travel in a straight line. As it slows down it tends to wobble and become inaccurate. If the target is a long way off, and if the gun or target is moving, then accuracy is even further reduced. Some of these problems have been solved by the development of efficient missiles which combine the high speed of rocket motors with the great accuracy of electronic guidance.

Launch of a TOW missile – an example of a modern precision-guided missile

TOW means tube-launched, optically-tracked, wire-guided. This cheap and simple-to-use weapon is very effective against tanks. After firing the missile, the gunner only has to keep the target in sight through the high-power binoculars on the launcher. As the missile heads for its target, it trails out two wires attached to the launcher and emits an infra-red light. A small computer on the launch vehicle compares the position of the target (which may be moving) to the position of the missile. If the missile is off course it sends instructions along the wires to move the fins on the missile so as to guide it precisely onto its target.

Weapons like TOW, which travel 3 km in 15 seconds, improve the ability of soldiers to withstand tank attacks, but during this time the soldier using TOW may be exposed to enemy fire, making its use risky. However, the latest generations of tanks are equipped with armour so strong that WOA missiles cannot penetrate them.

More complicated, more advanced, more expensive . . . but does it work?

A major feature of the arms race, particularly in the West, has been a constant drive for increasingly advanced technology in weaponry. Below are some examples of developments in weapons systems since 1916:

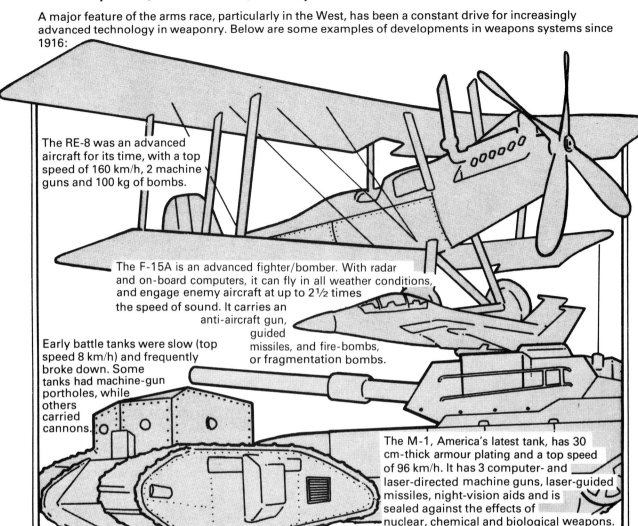

The RE-8 was an advanced aircraft for its time, with a top speed of 160 km/h, 2 machine guns and 100 kg of bombs.

The F-15A is an advanced fighter/bomber. With radar and on-board computers, it can fly in all weather conditions, and engage enemy aircraft at up to 2½ times the speed of sound. It carries an anti-aircraft gun, guided missiles, and fire-bombs, or fragmentation bombs.

Early battle tanks were slow (top speed 8 km/h) and frequently broke down. Some tanks had machine-gun portholes, while others carried cannons.

The M-1, America's latest tank, has 30 cm-thick armour plating and a top speed of 96 km/h. It has 3 computer- and laser-directed machine guns, laser-guided missiles, night-vision aids and is sealed against the effects of nuclear, chemical and biological weapons.

The technological fix

Modern advanced weapons systems are meant to be far more effective than those they replace. Some are, such as the heat-seeking guided missiles that can be used against tanks and aircraft. But in many cases, high-technology weapons turn out to be very costly and unreliable.

Less reliable

The F-15A, for all its advanced equipment, requires much more maintenance than simpler aircraft and so is more frequently grounded for repairs. Its electronic systems give away its position to enemy aircraft. In tests, much less sophisticated aircraft have been able to perform a lot better in the air. Similarly the M-1 tank has a lot of very delicate equipment which often goes wrong. It consumes nearly 2½ gallons of fuel per kilometre and it needs a complete new transmission after a few hundred kilometres. In battle the M-1 tank has to be accompanied by tankers, diggers and repair crews with spares, making it less effective.

Similar problems have beset the sophisticated cruise missile which in early trials embarrassed its manufacturers by losing its way and crashing into tall objects.

These kinds of problem have led some people to question whether all this complex technology will actually work efficiently in the heat of battle. The Americans, for all their computer technology, were beaten in Vietnam by opponents using inferior equipment. Warsaw Pact countries are equipped with larger quantities of less advanced equipment.

Soaring costs

The M-1 costs (in real terms) at least 7 times more than a typical Second World War tank, the F-15A is well over 100 times more expensive than its 1945 cousin. These soaring costs have demanded increasing resources for the arms race, but have brought fewer, more expensive weapons which may be less reliable than those they have replaced.

Using remote control to attack behind enemy lines

One ET system in development is MLRS (multiple launch rocket system). A remotely-piloted vehicle (1) sends back information about the target area. Rockets (2) are launched. These dispense sub-munitions (3) which then can home in on moving targets using radar guidance (4). Their range is up to 30 km.

Fixed targets can be attacked using LOCPODS (low-cost powered dispensers). These are fired from an aircraft (5) well away from the target. They approach using inertial navigation. When in the target area, they dispense large numbers of sub-munitions which can be used, for example, to crater a runway. Systems which can strike targets located much deeper within enemy territory are also being planned.

Such weapons are now available to most of the world's armies, navies and air forces. They are relatively cheap, very reliable and can be launched from ships, submarines, fighters and bombers as well as from special ground launchers. Many different guidance systems can be used. In addition to the infra-red system used by TOW there are heat-seeking missiles which lock onto engine exhausts. These can be very effective against aircraft. Other systems use laser beams or even TV cameras mounted in the nose of the missile which enable the launcher to direct it.

Emerging technology

Considerable effort is going into designing new types of precision-guided weapons, and defensive systems against them. These new systems – known collectively as *emerging technology* (ET) – can operate over distances exceeding 100 kilometres from the launch position. Their development has made it possible to fight battles over much greater distances than before. One possible strategy being considered by NATO commanders for using these new systems is to attack the reinforcements, supplies and communications behind the front lines of a Warsaw Pact attack without risking valuable aircraft and pilots in bombing raids.

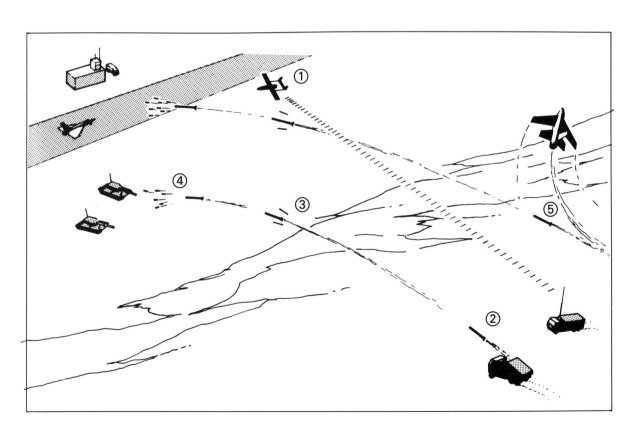

The missile age

The rocket motor is another important result of steady technological improvement. German scientists first developed rockets during the Second World War. One of these, called the V-2, was a *ballistic missile*. This term refers to weapons that are hurled up into the air by powerful rocket motors. When the motors burn out they fall away and the remaining part of the missile – the warhead containing the explosive – falls back to earth. Ballistic missiles play a very important part in modern warfare. There are many kinds of ballistic missiles ranging from ones that can travel only a few kilometres to those that can go half-way round the earth. Some are in fixed launching pads (called *silos* if they are underground), while others are on mobile launchers. Some are land-based, while others are launched from submarines. Some have warheads containing conventional explosives; others have nuclear warheads of various sizes. Earlier nuclear missiles carried just one warhead, but most modern nuclear missiles carry between three and fourteen separate warheads. Earlier ballistic missiles were not very accurate either. Modern nuclear missiles can be fitted with re-entry vehicles that, while still in space, can adjust their flightpath and shoot off several warheads at a number of widely separated targets with great accuracy (see the example of the *Minuteman III* missile on page 20). The new American *Pershing II* missile, fitted with a radar-homing warhead, is designed to be even more accurate. As it falls back to earth this compares a radar image of the target with an image stored in its computer memory. It should then be able to adjust its flight path so as to hit its target with pin-point accuracy after a journey of 1600 kilometres.

Recent developments in guidance mechanisms, computer technology and small efficient jet engines have led to the increased importance of the *cruise missile*. Like ballistic missiles, cruise missiles date back to the Second World War when German scientists developed the 'doodlebug' or 'flying bomb', a small winged missile that could carry a high-explosive warhead in a straight line for as long as its fuel lasted. These early missiles were very inaccurate and rarely hit any important targets. Royal Air Force pilots used to fly alongside the German V-1s and tip them up with the wings of their aircraft so that they would turn and fly harmlessly out to sea. After the war both the Americans and Russians developed new cruise missiles.

The American *Tomahawk* cruise missile is the product of recent technological developments. Its small efficient jet engine can carry it at 800 km/h over distances of up to 2500 kilometres. But its real usefulness lies in its specially developed guidance mechanisms. The missile carries a computer which is programmed with maps of the ground it will travel over. By comparing the actual position of the missile with its pre-set route the computer can pull it back on course. The computer is designed to enable the cruise missile to follow a zig-zag course very close to the ground (as low as fifteen metres). This makes it hard to track by radar and hard to knock out. As it approaches its target, radar in the nose of the missile compares the target area with its computer memory. This would enable it to 'home in' to its target with great accuracy. However, in the early stages of development of the cruise missile there were problems. While being tested several missiles crashed or flew off course in unpredictable directions. But at $1 million each, these missiles are

Different types of missiles

A *missile* is a weapon that is hurled at its target. A *ballistic missile* is launched into space by rocket motors. When these run out of fuel the remains of the missile fall back to earth. A *guided missile*, driven along by a rocket motor, is guided towards its target by various command signals that steer it. These can be carried by radar, radio, TV, trailing wires or on laser beams. If the missile has a programmed computer on board and systems to measure its speed, direction and height, it can steer itself. This is what a *cruise missile* does.

The warhead on a missile is the part which explodes and does the damage. Some missile carry conventional warheads, others carry nuclear warheads, and some missiles can carry either. Modern ballistic missiles carry several warheads each of which can be guided to a separate target. The very latest warheads use radar or satellite *terminal guidance* to direct them onto their targets as they approach them. This system is also employed in the cruise missile.

How the cruise missile works

1 Cruise missile launched from an aircraft, ship, submarine or ground-launcher.
2 The missile follows a low zig-zag path avoiding enemy defences and keeping out of the range of defensive radar.
3 The missile's special guidance system contains computerised maps of the ground over which the missile will travel.
4 Final homing radar locks the missile onto its target which it can expect to hit within a radius of 20 metres. This is important for destroying concrete hardened military targets even though it has a 200 kiloton warhead equal to 16 Hiroshima bombs.

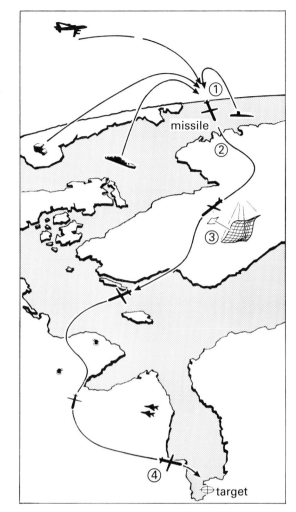

cheap in military terms and so it would be possible to use them in large numbers to swamp an enemy's defences. Expensive aircraft, ships and submarines can be kept well away from danger, while the cruise missiles fly to their targets – probably the enemy's airfields, military bases and command, control and intelligence installations.

During the 1980s, the Americans have been fitting large numbers of nuclear-armed cruise missiles to bomber aircraft, ships and submarines. A supersonic cruise missile is also being developed for deployment in the 1990s. The Russians are also beginning to produce cruise missiles that may be as capable as the American ones.

Space weapons

Satellites

Since 1957, more than two thousand satellites have been launched into orbit around the earth. About seventy-five per cent of them were put up there for military purposes. Some can carry cameras which can view the earth in very great detail. They may

The US 'Minuteman' – a modern long-range ballistic missile (ICBM)

The USA has 1000 Minuteman missiles widely scattered across country in underground silos protected by thick concrete shields. Each missile can reach targets 11 000 km away within about half an hour of being launched, travelling at a top speed of 24 000 km/h.

There has been a constant effort to improve the accuracy and destructiveness of the Minuteman missiles. This has been achieved by placing multiple warheads in the re-entry vehicles on the top of the missile. This is known as a MIRV (multiple, independently targeted re-entry vehicle). Before launch, the guidance system on the re-entry vehicle

(a small computer) can be programmed to shoot off each of the warheads at separate, widely spaced targets. Before the re-entry vehicle falls back to earth the guidance system plots its position against stars or satellites so that the warheads can be fired off at exactly the right time to hit their targets with great accuracy. The re-entry vehicle is equipped with small motors which enable it to adjust its flight path if necessary. 550 Minutemen are currently MIRVed. Of these, some 300 carry Mark 12A re-entry vehicles, with 3 × 335 kiloton warheads each of which can hit a target with the force of 26 Hiroshima bombs.

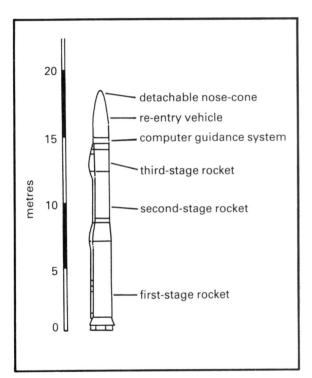

Fitting a new re-entry vehicle to a Minuteman missile

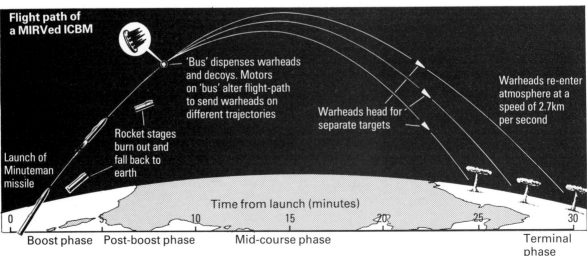

easily be used to keep an eye on the enemy's troop movements, unusual construction projects and new buildings, although they could equally well be used to check a country's compliance with any disarmament agreements. Any missile launch can be detected at once. At night or in cloudy conditions, infra-red cameras are used.

Satellites have become very important for relaying communications, especially between military commanders and their forces, wherever they may be. Satellites in fixed orbit are now being used to enable ships, submarines and aircraft to fix their positions with very great accuracy. This is important for navigation at night or in difficult weather. It is also crucial for nuclear missiles, since accurate targeting can only be achieved if the exact starting position is known, and if corrections to the flight-path can be made during the journey to the target.

In a war these satellites would be important targets, for once they had been knocked out, the military commanders would be severely handicapped. The superpowers are investing a great deal of time and money in developing ways of attacking each other's satellites. The Russians have launched many 'hunter-killer' satellites which could be moved near an enemy satellite and then exploded. The Americans are developing lasers which can be fired from high-altitude aircraft or put into space by the Space Shuttle. The American system is faster and more flexible than the Soviet one.

Star Wars

Recent technological developments have accelerated the arms race in space. Not only have communications and spy satellites been deployed there, but in 1983, the Americans announced plans to research and develop a defensive screen against incoming ballistic missiles. The proper name of this project is the *Strategic Defense Initiative* (SDI for short), but, because it will involve a great deal of space-age technology which does not yet exist, it has acquired the popular nickname 'Star Wars'.

In announcing the plans, the US President painted a picture of Star Wars as eventually (in the next century) providing a complete defence for the American population against a Soviet missile attack. He offered it as an attractive alternative to a defence programme which simply threatened to destroy millions of innocent people in retaliation for an attack.

Critics of Star Wars have argued that the project is hopelessly expensive and that it is impossible to achieve a totally effective shield that would destroy every one of thousands of incoming warheads before they could reach their targets. They argue that all that may eventually be possible is a defensive screen to protect the United States' ICBMs. But such a system, involving large space-based battle stations, laser mirrors and the like, would itself be extremely vulnerable to attack.

It can also be argued that the Russians will see Star Wars as a system that would allow the Americans to launch a surprise attack and then protect themselves against Soviet retaliation. They can be expected to react by deploying increased numbers of missiles – especially large ICBMs with lots of warheads – in an attempt to overwhelm US defences. Thus, rather than help to make the USA safe from nuclear weapons, Star Wars may contribute to increasing the dangers to the whole world of a still greater build-up of nuclear forces and greater Soviet suspicion of US intentions.

'Stars Wars' scenario

The diagram shows how a layered defence system against ballistic missile attack might work. For simplicity, the diagram only shows single missiles. In reality there might be thousands involved. Similarly, there would be many more Star Wars platforms. The four layers of the defence might be as follows:

An early-warning satellite (1) picks up the rocket launch. The first layer of defence is a chemical laser (2) which attacks rockets as they are climbing through the earth's atmosphere. In the second layer, the 'bus' which dispenses the warheads and decoys is attacked by an electro-magnetic railgun (3). In the mid-course phase of the defence, a target-acquisition and tracking satellite (4) locates and passes on information about the surviving warheads so that they can be attacked by, for example, another laser (5). The fourth layer is the terminal defence. In this, an infra-red probe (6) is sent into space to relay information about the paths of the remaining incoming warheads and to tell the difference between live warheads and decoys. The warheads are intercepted by non-nuclear devices (7) which, after launch by rocket, home in using infra-red heat-seeking sensors.

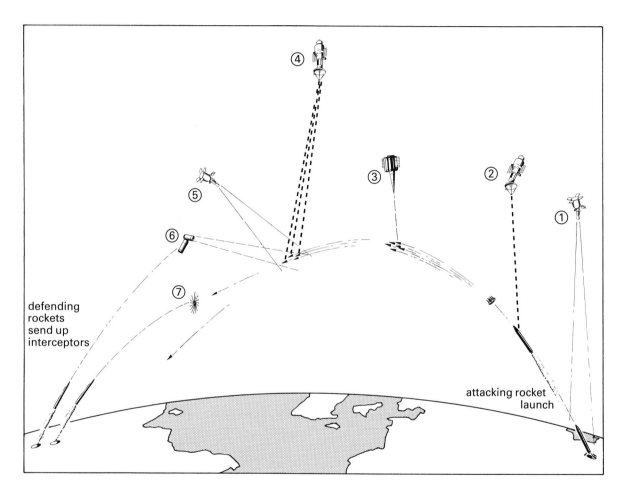

defending rockets send up interceptors

attacking rocket launch

Area weapons

It is not always possible to pinpoint a target such as a column of soldiers, a group of tanks or an ammunition dump which may cover a large area of ground. To strike such targets, much research has gone into the development of weapons that can devastate a huge area. As a result, most modern armed forces today are equipped with *cluster bombs* and fire-bombs.

A cluster bomb is a container holding between 600 and 900 small bombs. When dropped from an aircraft the container splits open, spreading the bombs over a very wide area. These can be fused to explode just above or at ground level. Each one sends out hundreds of jagged pieces of metal or ball bearings. These fragments, travelling at very high speeds, can tear through people, tyres, fuel tanks and so on.

A variation on the cluster bomb is the controlled use of fire. Fire has been used as a terror weapon for many centuries. The defenders of besieged cities in the Middle Ages would pour burning pitch upon their attackers. Flame-throwers were used in both world wars to fling burning petrol up to thirty-two metres towards a target. At the end of the Second World War, the USA developed a substance called *napalm*. This is essentially a thickened jelly-like form of petrol which burns at very high temperature and when dropped onto people sticks to them so that they cannot brush it off. Napalm can be dropped from specially-made tanks carried by aircraft. When ignited, napalm can blanket huge areas in a sea of fire. Because it burns for a very long time at such a high temperature people caught in a napalm drop suffer the most serious and agonising burns. Often the skin is burned right down to the bone. The United Nations have condemned the use of napalm as an exceptionally cruel weapon. But this has not prevented its continued use.

There are other ways of causing destruction over a wide area. One way is to explode chemicals which have been sprayed from an aircraft or dropped in a canister. This produces a devastating explosion over a very wide area. For example, an incredibly powerful bomb was developed for use in the Vietnam War in the 1960s. It was nicknamed the 'Daisy Cutter'. Weighing over 7000 kilos, it was floated down to earth on a parachute where its chemical mixture exploded with a force that flattened everything over a huge area of 1.5 hectares, and killed all living things (including even the worms in the ground). Anyone within that area would have had their lungs ruptured by the force of the explosion.

Only nuclear explosions are more powerful than that produced by the 'Daisy Cutter'. There are many small nuclear bombs and shells now available to the armed forces of the superpowers, which produce about the same explosive damage as the 'Daisy Cutter'. Some experts believe that the gap between conventional and nuclear weapons has now been narrowed, making it more thinkable for generals to start using nuclear weapons in a battle. But nuclear weapons have certain features which make them very different from all other weapons. And, in terms of their destructive power, nuclear weapons begin where other weapons leave off.

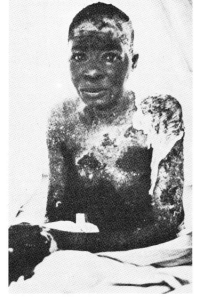

A victim of napalm.

Computer-controlled warfare

There have also been considerable improvements in computer technology to develop systems which can direct and control both conventional and nuclear warfare. The great complexity and speed of modern weapons systems of all kinds, and the vast distances over which wars might range (especially nuclear warfare) has meant that the power of modern computers to process large amounts of information extremely quickly has become an essential part of modern warfare.

On the smallest scale, computers are used to help pilots to fly their planes, to guide warheads to their targets, and to detect and confuse enemy forces. On the largest scale, defence computers can gather and analyse information about a nuclear attack, and prepare retaliatory forces for action.

Computers are now crucial elements in the complex systems that have been developed to control battles. Battle commanders now sit in front of VDU screens onto which information is flashed as soon as it comes in. The same system is used to transmit orders to military forces and to analyse the progress of the battle, including enemy strength and positions and damage incurred by the opposing forces.

As technology improves, it is possible that the amount of information will be so vast and the speed at which it has to be processed so great, that the computers will have to take decisions without human intervention about what to do, This might be the case with Star Wars, for example, when the decision to attack the Soviet Union might have to be made within one minute of a Soviet missile launch! Moreover, because fast and reliable communications are essential in any war, such facilities will be high-priority targets for any attack.

The arms race is increasingly becoming a race to improve technology. There are continuing efforts in both superpowers to produce ever more sophisticated weapons systems. The result has been to produce soaring costs, extremely complicated systems, and much less time for human beings to sort out and control military forces in a crisis.

In this chapter we have seen how important has been the part played by technological developments in the arms race. Much research and investment has gone into the design of weapons systems which are faster, more accurate, more deadly and more flexible than those they replace. This, of course, has also stimulated efforts to develop defences against these new developments. Thus, new, accurate guided-missiles have led to the introduction of anti-missile missiles to shoot them down, and electronic countermeasures to confuse the missiles' guidance systems. There is no end to this kind of race, for the next step is to produce an even more sophisticated missile which can get through the improved defences, and so on. Most, but not all, of these developments are more complicated and expensive than those they replace. As we shall see in the rest of the book, technological developments have been very important features of the nuclear arms race and among the major reasons for its continuation.

If both sides in a conflict have equal capabilities provided by their military forces it may be possible for them to balance each other and prevent fighting taking place. But, as we shall see, the availability of newer and more deadly weapons systems for sale throughout the world is a great temptation for military and political leaders in countries which want to get the better of their adversaries. And once fighting does break out, the new, modern weapons systems can mean that the war can move over very large distances very quickly and involve huge destruction and loss of life in a very short time. In these circumstances, the chances of the war escalating and getting out of control are much increased.

It may well be that the development of new, highly accurate precision-guided weapons now makes it possible for a country to defend itself against attack by greatly superior forces. As we shall see in the final chapter, an increasing number of people are arguing that countries could use this new technology in conventional weapons to defend themselves as an alternative to relying on nuclear weapons.

Who's winning the technology race?

	US ahead	Neck and neck	USSR ahead
Computers	✔		
Warheads (nuclear and conventional)		✔	
Lasers		✔	
Guidance and navigation	✔		
Advanced materials	✔		
Radar	✔		
Robotics	✔		
Submarine detection	✔		
Telecommunications	✔		

According to studies carried out by the US military, the Russians are behind the Americans in most of the technologies that are important for military purposes.

3 Weapons of mass destruction: nuclear, chemical and biological

Hiroshima

At 08.15 on the morning of 6 August 1945, an American atomic bomb exploded 580 metres above the Japanese city of Hiroshima. There was a blinding flash followed by a huge explosion. Within a second the bomb had turned into a huge fireball as hot as the inside of the sun, expanding to a width of 280 metres. The heat of the explosion simply evaporated people beneath it and burned to death others as far as 1.2 kilometres away. Up to four kilometres from the explosion people in the open received very serious burns. Within half an hour, two square kilometres of the city had become a raging inferno, as everything began to burn and the fires joined together to form one huge firestorm. By this time nearly 75 000 of Hiroshima's inhabitants were dead. As the heat rose, water vapour condensed around the ashes of people and other objects and then began to fall back to earth as a black rain.

The blast-wave (the wall of air pushed out by the heat of the explosion) moved out from the centre of the explosion at a speed of many hundreds of kilometres per hour. Within ten seconds it had travelled four kilometres. In the area two kilometres around the explosion nearly all buildings were flattened. Further out, many buildings were damaged beyond repair and thousands of people were injured by fragments of flying glass, collapsing buildings and flying metal and bricks.

The city of Hiroshima two months after the atomic explosion. It is still a total ruin. Only the shells of a few strong buildings remain; the rest is rubble. The white tracks are roads. Most modern nuclear weapons are far more destructive than the one that did this damage.

Three days after the bombing of Hiroshima, an atomic bomb was dropped on the Japanese city of Nagasaki. This photograph was taken soon after the bomb had exploded.

Nuclear explosions

groundburst
airburst

Nuclear bombs can be detonated at pre-set heights over their targets. A *groundburst* occurs when a nuclear explosion is close enough to the ground for the fireball to touch the ground. When this happens a crater is gouged out and huge amounts of material are sucked into the air, later to return to earth as fallout.

In an *airburst* the fireball does not touch the ground. The higher the explosion the wider the area of destruction caused by the bomb.

At the moment of the explosion the bomb gave off vast amounts of radiation, and further radiation continued to come from the bomb fragments and other debris for a long time afterwards. Those people who had survived within a two-kilometre area of the explosion, and rescuers who went into the city centre soon afterwards, began to complain of a mysterious illness a few days later. The worst-affected people began to feel very sick and to vomit blood. They suffered serious diarrhoea and began to bleed from the bowels, gums, nose and genitals. Their bodies came out in purple spots and their hair began to fall out. They became very weak. Wounds refused to heal. These are the symptoms of radiation sickness. Many of those who were affected by radiation died in great pain, days or weeks later.

Others slowly recovered. Many of these people developed cancers later in life and lived on in great pain until they suffered a premature death. Pregnant women exposed to radiation gave birth to deformed babies. Today there are still many thousands of people in Hiroshima suffering from the effects of the bomb. The death toll from that one nuclear bomb is still rising. More than 200 000 have already died; and more die each year from the long-term effects of the explosion.

In comparison with most of today's nuclear weapons, the Hiroshima bomb was a midget. Although it exploded with a power 2000 times greater than the heaviest blitz bombing of London in the Second World War, the Hiroshima bomb is dwarfed by most of today's weapons. The Minuteman missile carries three 335-kiloton warheads, each one twenty-five times bigger than the bomb which destroyed Hiroshima. The tiny cruise missile has a warhead equal to fifteen Hiroshima bombs. The largest nuclear test explosion (carried out by the Russians in 1961) was estimated to be 58 megatons or equal to 45 000 Hiroshima bombs.

Nuclear explosions

Nuclear explosions are different from all others. Conventional explosions result from chemical reactions which rapidly produce great amounts of hot gases. It is these gases which, contained for a brief moment within a shell, bullet or bomb, produce the explosion. As the gas expands it shatters its container, sending fragments flying at high speeds in all directions. It also pushes a wall of air before it. This is the blast-wave which travels outwards from the centre of the explosion, flattening objects in its path until its energy has gone. Most explosions kill by blast or by tearing their victims, though, as we have seen, fire-bombs work differently.

Nuclear explosions are produced either by breaking up or fusing together small quantities of radioactive elements. One such element is *uranium* which is a metal found in various parts of the world. Once it has been refined (see the diagram on page 39) it can be used to make a nuclear bomb. Another substance used in nuclear weapons is *plutonium* which can be obtained by 'burning' uranium in a nuclear reactor. When these elements are broken up or fused together in a particular way – as happens in a nuclear bomb – they give out a tremendous amount of energy: hence the huge power of a nuclear explosion. For example, half a kilogram of plutonium has the explosive power of 9 million kilograms of TNT (the chemical explosive trinitrotoluene).

There are, however, limits to the size of explosions that can be made by the breaking up (*fission*) of uranium or plutonium, because above certain weights (about 15 kg for uranium and 5 kg for plutonium) they can explode unpredictably. Therefore in atomic bombs the fission materials have to be kept separate until they are suddenly brought together for the intended explosion. Keeping the separate amounts small, however, means that the explosion in this kind of nuclear bomb is limited.

Just over seven years after the Hiroshima atomic bomb, American scientists developed a new kind of nuclear weapon known as the hydrogen (or *fusion*) bomb. This bomb uses the fission explosion of uranium to create the high temperature (several millions of degrees centigrade) needed to set off a process in which atoms of hydrogen are fused together to give off even greater amounts of energy. With this development the way was open to build bombs with bigger

---

Different types of nuclear bombs

atom bomb
hydrogen bomb
thermonuclear bomb

The *atomic bomb* or *atom bomb* refers to a bomb that explodes from the fission (breaking up) of uranium or plutonium. This is the simplest type of bomb, and was the type used on Hiroshima and Nagasaki.

Much bigger explosions can be achieved in *hydrogen bombs* where a fission explosion is used to set off a fusion of hydrogen atoms, resulting in an enormous release of energy. Even bigger explosions can be produced by blanketing the fusion bomb with quantities of stable uranium, which in turn creates a further large fission explosion. All this happens in a split second. Most modern nuclear bombs are of this type. This kind of bomb is also called *thermonuclear* because of the high temperature needed for fusion.

Nuclear explosions

Nuclear explosions are expressed in terms of how much TNT (the chemical explosive trinitrotoluene) would be needed to make a similar explosion. So a 1 kiloton (1 kt) nuclear explosion is equivalent to 1000 tonnes of TNT. A 1 megaton (1 Mt) nuclear explosion is equivalent to 1 million tonnes of TNT.

How a thermonuclear bomb works

bomb casing

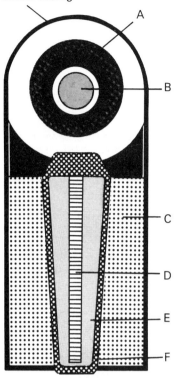

A high explosive 'trigger'

B uranium and plutonium core

C polystyrene foam

D plutonium 'plug'

E lithium/deuterium capsule

F uranium-238 casing

This is how one version of a thermonuclear bomb works: Electrical signals set off high explosives (A). This explosion compresses the core (B) which fissions. The heat given off by this explosion sets off another one. The foam (C) explodes and compresses the plug (D) which fissions. This sets off a fusion explosion in the capsule (E) which in turn sets off a further massive fission explosion in the uranium casing (F). The whole chain reaction, from (A) to (F), takes place in only a fraction of a second. Using this design, massive explosions can be produced from small amounts of materials. Therefore bombs can be lighter, smaller and cheaper.

explosive yield while reducing the size of the warhead. There is no theoretical upper limit to the size of these *thermonuclear* weapons.

Another feature of nuclear explosions which makes them different from all others is that, in the explosion, bursts of ionising radiation are given out. This kind of radiation consists of extremely small particles or energy waves which cannot be detected by the human senses. In the smallest quantities they are very dangerous; in larger quantities they can lead to death since they can pass through solid objects and can enter the body and cause the body cells to die or break down. The radiation effects of nuclear explosions are greatest in the few seconds of an explosion. But they linger on in the debris of the bomb, the dust and fragments of buildings, soil and anything which is enveloped by the fireball. All these particles become radioactive and give off dangerous radiation for days, weeks or even years after the explosion. The falling back to earth of radioactive particles sucked into the air by a groundburst is known as *radioactive fallout*.

Since 1945 the nuclear weapons states have set off more than 1500 nuclear explosions. Most of these have been underground but quite a few have been in the atmosphere. These explosions have been a part of the testing and development of new nuclear warheads. Using the information available from these explosions and from the known effects of the bombing of Hiroshima and Nagasaki, it is possible to work out the likely effects of nuclear explosions in a nuclear war.

In the following pages, in an effort to give some idea of the immense destructive power of nuclear weapons, we have set out the likely results of a one-megaton nuclear bomb on Leicester, a medium-sized city in the middle of England and a possible target in the event of a nuclear war. The effects of the bomb on Leicester would be influenced by several things. Much would depend, for example, on whether the bomb was *ground-* or *air-burst*. If it were raining or foggy the heat effects would be reduced. The extent and amount of the fallout descending in any particular place would depend on the strength and direction of the wind, and upon whether or not it was raining. If the attack came at night fewer people would be out in the open and therefore flash burns might be less. If there were advance warning of attack, people might have time to get into underground shelters (if there were any), or to build makeshift shelters in their homes, as shown in the government pamphlet *Protect and Survive*, or to escape from the city altogether. The final death toll would also depend upon whether the attack on Leicester was an isolated one or part of a general attack upon Britain. In the former event, rescue would soon be at hand for people in the outlying districts. Those who were injured might be moved to hospitals elsewhere. Those who were trapped might be rescued. But it is much more likely that Leicester would be only one among perhaps 150 targets throughout Britain. In that event there would be no help and no rescue. The survivors would be left to fend for themselves as best they could. Fires would burn out of control. Injuries would receive no attention. Those trapped would be left to die. Electricity, water and gas supplies would all be cut. This picture might be repeated all over Britain – perhaps all over Europe, North America and the Soviet Union.

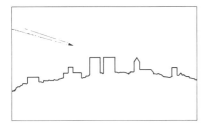

The single warhead aimed at Leicester explodes 200 metres above the Central Post Office.

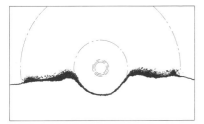

Within one second the city centre is engulfed by a fireball whose temperature reaches 10 million degrees centigrade. In another 9 seconds, the fireball expands to 2700 metres across and rises rapidly. Everything caught within the fireball is vaporised, and a huge crater is carved out under the centre of the explosion. The tremendous heat sets fire to things for many kilometres around. It also produces a blast wave that smashes everything in its path up to nearly 3 kilometres from the centre of the explosion.

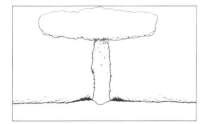

After 10 minutes, the fireball has cooled and has sucked thousands of tons of earth and debris as high as 19 kilometres into the atmosphere. The cooling fireball forms a mushroom cloud of water vapour and debris 16 kilometres across. The heavier objects sucked up by the explosion begin to fall back to earth at once. The lighter particles drift on the wind and float back to earth hours, days or weeks later. All these particles are highly radioactive. Fallout can kill.

What one nuclear bomb could do

These diagrams show the effects of a single one megaton bomb detonated above the centre of an average-sized city. The city of Leicester, population 2 86 000, is used as an example but a number of other cities would have done just as well.

1 Heat and blast – at the centre

The tremendous forces unleashed by the explosion produce a zone of total destruction over an area of about 2.7 kilometres radius from the centre of the explosion – 'Ground Zero'. Within this zone nearly everything above ground level is obliterated. The heat of the explosion and winds of more than 500 km/h cause tremendous damage: metals melt, steel buildings and motor vehicles liquidise. Concrete buildings collapse. Near the centre of the explosion people and solid objects simply evaporate. A crater 65 metres deep and 300 metres across is gouged out around the centre of the explosion. A 16-storey building could be fitted into this hole. Around the crater a ring of debris 15 metres high is deposited out to a distance of 30 metres from Ground Zero.

Further out, buildings are smashed flat. Everything that can burn is on fire. People are killed by suffocation, by appalling burns, by falling masonry.

Nearly everyone in the area shown below will be killed, and for a further 2 kilometres outwards about 98 per cent of the population will die from the immediate effects of the heat and blast. This adds up to 170 000 people. Everything you can see in this photograph will be destroyed.

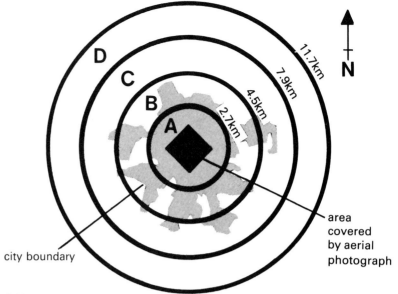

Reconstruction of what happens to brick structures within Zone B. The house (above) is first set on fire by the heat of the fireball. A few seconds later the blast wave arrives and completely demolishes it (below).

city boundary

area covered by aerial photograph

2 Heat and blast – further out

Zone B
Zone of severe damage. Rubber and plastics melt and catch fire. Wood chars and burns. Trees are knocked down. Cars are overturned by winds of between 250 and 500 km/h – several times more powerful than a hurricane. People caught in the open are severely burned and crushed by falling buildings and flying glass. Fires break out everywhere. Streets are blocked with debris. There are many serious injuries among survivors, with possibly 100 000 people requiring urgent medical attention. In this zone 50 per cent of the population would be dead and 40 per cent injured from the blast effects alone.

Zone C
Zone of 'moderate' damage. In this zone houses are left standing though tiles and windows are blown out. Curtains, clothing and upholstery catch fire. People caught in the open receive third degree burns which require intensive medical treatment.

Zone D
Zone of 'light' damage. Windows are smashed and some brickwork is damaged. Flying glass, bricks and stones are still very dangerous. People caught in the open may receive second degree blister burns. These could kill if they do not receive sterile medical attention.

A victim of third degree burns, which people caught in the open in Zone C are likely to suffer. The skin is charred to the bone. If burns like these cover more than 10 per cent of the body area the victim is likely to die of infection and fluid loss.

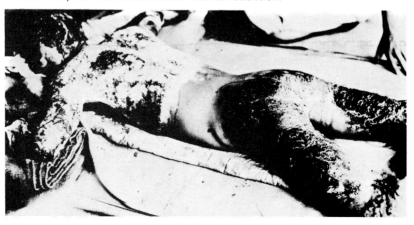

3 The fallout pattern – 6 weeks afterwards

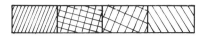

Radiation dose received by unprotected people during the 6 weeks following the explosion

Zone 1: > 4000 RADS
In this zone unprotected people feel the severe effects of radiation sickness within hours of the explosion. Severe and disabling illness is followed rapidly by death. Only those in purpose-built underground shelters can be sure to survive.

Zone 2: > 1300 RADS
Unprotected people in this zone are likely to die within a fortnight. Makeshift indoor shelters with outside doors and windows bricked up might aid survival if the house is not seriously damaged. Serious illness is however very likely.

Zone 3: > 440 RADS
At least half the people receiving this dose suffer severe and painful illness and then die. Survivors may yet die of simple infections and have high risk of cancer. Simple indoor shelters offer considerable protection.

Zone 4: > 130 RADS
Survival in this zone is likely, though most people will be extremely ill for some time and many will later develop cancer. Many babies will be born deformed.

What protection is there from radiation?

Radiation is absorbed by thick solid objects such as soil, concrete, lead and brick. Shielding of such materials can give protection provided that air intakes are filtered and there are no cracks in the shield.

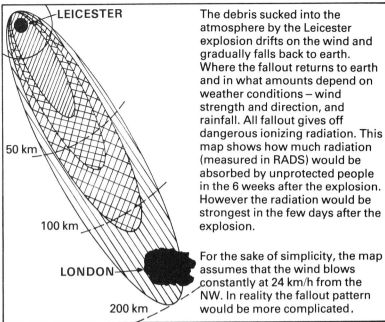

The debris sucked into the atmosphere by the Leicester explosion drifts on the wind and gradually falls back to earth. Where the fallout returns to earth and in what amounts depend on weather conditions – wind strength and direction, and rainfall. All fallout gives off dangerous ionizing radiation. This map shows how much radiation (measured in RADS) would be absorbed by unprotected people in the 6 weeks after the explosion. However the radiation would be strongest in the few days after the explosion.

For the sake of simplicity, the map assumes that the wind blows constantly at 24 km/h from the NW. In reality the fallout pattern would be more complicated.

What does radiation do?

Radioactive fallout settles as a dust on buildings, trees and the ground. It gives off dangerous ionising radiation for weeks, months or years after the explosion. In all but the very lowest doses this kind of radiation is dangerous to humans. It is invisible. It can pass through solid objects and enter the body. There is no cure for radiation sickness, though blood transfusions and bone marrow transplants may save some people who might otherwise die.

Radiation sickness

Depending on the dose received the victim suffers from vomiting and diarrhoea, and severe fatigue. Later symptoms include loss of hair, internal bleeding, and bleeding from the genitals, ulceration and fever. Death follows or there is a long, painful recovery. Long-term effects include a high risk of cancer.

RADIATION ENTERS THE BODY
by being eaten on contaminated food or in contaminated water or by being breathed in

by passing through plastic and cloth to damage or kill body cells

by affecting exposed parts of the body

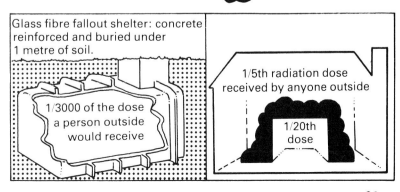

Glass fibre fallout shelter: concrete reinforced and buried under 1 metre of soil.

1/3000 of the dose a person outside would receive

1/5th radiation dose received by anyone outside

1/20th dose

Chemical weapons

We have not yet finished our catalogue of military hardware that nations have built up since the Second World War. Perhaps nothing can compete with the terrible power of nuclear weapons, but the availability of lethal chemicals and germs is yet another part of modern warfare and the result of much research effort.

Chemical weapons were first used very effectively in the First World War. Initially, casualties were very high. The first German attack on French lines injured 10 000 men and killed another 5000. In all there were one million casualties of gas warfare in the First World War. Since then technological developments in chemical warfare have produced gases which are very effective against unprotected people. Only a small amount needs to be breathed in or to touch the skin for the victim to collapse and die.

In 1925 most major countries in the world signed the *Geneva Protocol* which banned the use of poison chemicals as weapons. However, many countries, including the USSR, USA, France, Britain and China reserved the right to retaliate using chemical weapons if another country broke the agreement and used them first. This allowed some countries to continue to produce chemical weapons for 'defensive' purposes. Despite the Geneva Protocol, the superpowers in particular have built up huge stocks of poison chemicals and the necessary systems for using them. In 1969 the Americans ceased producing and stockpiling chemical weapons and entered into talks with the Russians about a complete ban on production of such weapons. No agreement had been reached by the mid 1980s. Pressure was rising within the USA to restart production and create a modern stockpile in order to match Soviet forces.

In the late 1930s new, more powerful chemical agents were discovered. The most minute quantities (about 0.4 milligram, or less than a grain of salt) of these so called *nerve gases* produce almost immediate collapse and death. The Americans have stockpiled over 10 000 tonnes of nerve gases. To deliver these nerve gases they have nearly 1.5 million shells, 13 000 bombs and about nine hundred 720-litre aircraft spray tanks. There is no precise knowledge of Soviet stocks, but some Western estimates credit them with larger quantities, perhaps as high as 300 000 tonnes.

All NATO and Warsaw Pact forces are equipped to protect themselves against chemical weapons. Soldiers are issued with complete protective suits, gas masks and syringes to enable them to

American stockpiles of Sarin and VX nerve gases

Each drum contains about 720 litres of nerve gas. One milligram of Sarin is enough to kill an adult. There are two major problems with these stocks: they are in the wrong place, thousands of kilometres away from Europe where they are supposed to be used. Also, drums like these may gradually corrode and leak, releasing their deadly contents into the atmosphere.

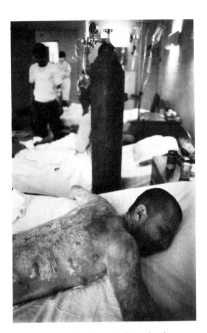

An Iranian victim of chemical weapons. Such weapons have been extensively used by Iraq in the Iran–Iraq war.

give themselves an antidote if caught unawares. All modern tanks and many other military vehicles can be completely sealed from the outside environment. This gives considerable protection against not only poison chemicals but also against nuclear fallout and germ warfare.

In 1986, the US Congress gave approval for the production of new nerve gas shells to replace the current stocks. These, known as binaries, mix together during flight to produce lethal gas. They are thus much safer to handle than the old type which were liable to corrode and to leak after a long period of storage.

The Americans plan to manufacture 1.2 million binary shells and 44 000 spraybombs to carry nerve gases. These would contain some 9000 tonnes of chemicals. They could be deployed in Europe at a time of international tension. A single drop of such a chemical can kill an unprotected person; a quantity about the size of a sugar cube could kill 2500.

Apart from the failure to agree a ban on chemical weapons, and the US decision to produce binary weapons, the most serious development in the 1980s has been the use of chemical weapons by Iraq in its war with Iran. More than 10 000 soldiers have been killed or wounded by poison gas in this war. It has been reported that, in 1986, Iraq had begun to manufacture several tonnes of nerve gas each month at a secret factory. This is likely to spur a chemical arms race in the Middle East unless it can be halted. There is evidence that several countries in the Middle East – among them Syria, Libya and Israel – possess and may be able to make chemical weapons.

Biological weapons

In earlier centuries one way of bringing the citizens of besieged cities to their knees was to throw the corpses of people who had died of the plague over the city walls in order to spread that disease among the trapped people. In the last century, there were many cases of American Indians being given presents in the form of blankets impregnated with smallpox germs by the white settlers. Modern germ warfare is merely a development of these practices. The attraction of using germs is their potential for causing widespread disruption and death among enemy populations. Because germs multiply and spread when in contact with live animals and humans, only a small amount – put in the water supply or injected into rats or other rodents – would be more than enough to start an epidemic. However, military leaders do not think that germ warfare would be very useful. They prefer precise and predictable weapons and the progress of a disease could not be predicted. It might infect the wrong people and rage out of control across the world. Since germs have not proved very useful in warfare, despite much research carried out this century, it was not too difficult to negotiate a total ban on the development, production or storing of biological weapons and missiles. All major countries in the world have signed the *Biological Weapons Convention* of 1972. Nevertheless, biological weapons could be an awful weapon in the hands of terrorists. It is clear that the strictest controls must be placed on germ research and upon the handling of dangerous bacteria.

4 The arms trade

Arms exporters, 1981–85

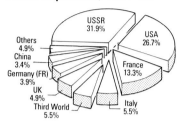

Eighty per cent of all arms exports come from the rich industrialised countries. The USA and Soviet Union together account for nearly 60 per cent of world arms sales. But Third World countries (like Israel and Brazil) are producing and exporting an increasing number of weapons themselves. They are manufactured on machinery supplied by the main arms exporting countries.

Main arms importing regions, 1981–85

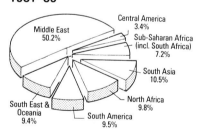

The war-torn Middle East absorbs half of the world's arms trade. Altogether the Third World imports about 60 per cent of all traded weapons.

Source: *SIPRI*

On the average day during the decade 1970–80 there were fourteen wars in progress somewhere in the world. Since the end of the Second World War there has not been one day when the whole world has been at peace. Since 1945 there have been about 120 wars in which more than 30 million people have died. Nearly all these wars have been fought in the less industrialised, poorer parts of the world. In most cases these wars were fought using weapons supplied by the richer industrialised nations, including the Soviet Union. The world arms trade is big business, amounting to a staggering $37 billion in 1983. The Americans used to be the world's biggest suppliers, but recently the Russians have overtaken them. In third place comes France; then, a long way behind come the United Kingdom, West Germany, Czechoslovakia, Italy and China.

The amount and cost of armaments from these supplying countries have been rising very steeply since 1970. More and more of the world's poorer countries have begun to import advanced weapons from abroad. Many of them have received expensive, modern aircraft such as the American F-15 and the Soviet MIG-23. The most advanced precision-guided weapons have also been sold or given to a wide range of countries. Only five per cent of the arms trade is organised by private dealers. They deal mainly in older small guns and ammunition. All the remaining arms transfers are from one government to another.

Suppliers and buyers

There are many reasons why the industrialised countries supply weapons abroad. The two superpowers and the European arms exporters are involved in the trade for different reasons. For the superpowers, the transfer of weapons to friendly countries can be a good way of defending their own interests and of projecting their power abroad. To the leaders of the two superpowers, the whole world is a matter of concern. The Americans and the Russians are in competition with each other for power and influence. They also both believe that, in order to protect their trading and political interests throughout the world, they must be strong military powers themselves and must be prepared to support countries friendly to them. They believe that the arms trade is an effective method of achieving these aims.

By supplying weapons on 'easy terms' to poorer countries, the superpowers often seek military facilities such as harbours, airports and military bases for their forces in return. Such facilities enable the armed forces of the superpowers to operate throughout the globe and they both now have a number of bases and harbours in various countries. Each superpower has increasingly used other countries to try to reduce the influence of the other in various parts of the world. For example, the Russians have supplied weapons and advisers to Angola to oppose US influence, while the Americans have supplied military equipment to Saudi Arabia to reduce Soviet influence in that area. The Americans are usually keen to provide weapons for governments who declare themselves opposed to the spread of Soviet communism (for example South Korea, El Slavador, Pakistan and Israel). The Russians are willing to support 'liberation movements' fighting to overthrow Western-style capitalist governments and they supply large amounts of weapons to socialist countries opposed to the USA (such as Cuba, Libya, South Yemen). Both superpowers will also supply weapons to countries (such as India) simply to keep them out of the hands of the other power.

The arms trade has many benefits for the superpowers. In some cases selling arms can be very profitable, while in other cases the supply of weapons at 'knock-down' prices is done primarily for political reasons. The oil-rich countries of the Middle East account for about thirty per cent of world arms sales. They are very important customers since they have, in many cases, been able to pay cash on delivery. This helps the superpowers and other exporters to cover the huge costs of weapons' production. But many importing countries are less well off. They often have to borrow the money to buy their weapons, though if they are very important countries to the superpowers (for example an important ally), they may get the weapons they want on very easy terms or even free, as a form of economic aid.

As we have said, the superpowers are keen to increase their influence and control throughout the world. The arms trade can make the importing countries dependent on the supplying nation. The advanced weapons systems they receive need careful use and maintenance. Therefore hundreds or even thousands of technicians and 'advisers', often from the military, go out with the weapons. The importing countries also have to rely on the exporters for their supplies of spare parts, and so the exporting nations can use this dependence to exert political influence. But the arms trade does not always work in the supplier's interest. The superpowers cannot always use the arms trade as a lever to control the countries to whom they supply weapons. For example, in 1972 President Sadat

". . . And for firing single rounds you just flip this little thing here."

The F-5E fighter/bomber, made in the USA, has been sold in large numbers to many Third World countries including Iran, Chile, Taiwan, Saudi Arabia and South Korea. The photograph shows the range of weapons that can be carried by the F-5E.

of Egypt expelled thousands of Russian military advisers from the country and began to turn to the USA for friendship. In 1980, Iran (a country which by the late 1970s was buying half of *all* US arms exports) had a revolution which deposed the pro-American Shah and replaced him with a very anti-American government. In 1982 during a dispute with Argentina over control of the Falkland Islands, British servicemen had to face attacks from weapons which had been supplied to Argentina by British governments.

Feeding the war machine

As weapons suppliers, the superpowers can easily be dragged into other people's wars. In 1973, for example, in the Middle East, the Arabs and Israelis fought a short but intense war. For several days, each side suffered very heavy losses of both aircraft and tanks. Both superpowers mounted massive airlifts of spares and replacements for the weapons they had supplied. When the war ended the destroyed weapons and losses were made up by the superpowers. The war could not have continued without superpower support, but neither wished to see their side lose.

When war broke out in 1980 between Iran and Iraq, initially both the USA and Soviet Union refused to supply any weapons or spares. If all countries had followed suit the war would have ground to a halt within weeks or months as both sides ran out of usable weapons. But this did not happen. Over forty countries have supplied weapons to the warring countries. The superpowers have been involved in supplying *both* sides, as have most of the other major arms-exporting countries. These actions have fuelled and prolonged a bitter war in which hundreds of thousands of people have died.

Some governments use imported military hardware to oppress their own people. Many dictatorial governments in Latin America use weapons supplied by countries such as the USA, Israel, France, Germany and Britain in this way. In this photograph, anti-government suspects are being rounded up for questioning in El Salvador by soldiers armed with West German Heckler and Koch G-3 rifles.

In many parts of the world (such as the Middle East, South East Asia, southern Africa and in India and Pakistan) the willingness of industrial countries to supply the weapons demanded by Third World governments has led to local arms races. The supply of advanced weapons to one country in a region simply helps to make its neighbours feel threatened. They build up their weapons, forcing other neighbouring countries to follow suit. So in this way an ever rising spiral of a weapons build-up is created.

The European arms-exporting countries are less interested in gaining influence abroad and more interested in making money. As a rule they will supply weapons to any government that can pay, even if those weapons would fuel a local arms race (as in the Middle East) or be used by dictatorial governments against their own people (as in South Africa, El Salvador or Chile). The sale of arms to foreign governments is the only way in which European countries can keep their arms industries going. They need to sell large numbers of arms each year to make production profitable. They could not survive by supplying only their own armed forces. Therefore the French, Italians and British in particular try very hard to sell their military goods throughout the world. Only in this way can the jobs of the 500 000 employees in Britain and 300 000 in France who depend on the arms industry for their livelihood be preserved.

Even so, jobs in the arms industries are not secure. Cancellation of orders can immediately throw people out of work. There are several studies which suggest that more people could be employed by investing money in other industries or services. It has been estimated that for every ten jobs created in defence, thirteen could have been created (with the same amount of money) in the National Health Service in Britain, for example, or in the construction industry.

The result of the growing world trade in weaponry is to make the world a more dangerous and war-like place. An increasing number of the world's poorer countries have spent a large proportion of their limited incomes on armaments, instead of investing in agriculture and industry. Many vicious and dictatorial military governments are kept in power by the weapons supplied by the arms-exporting countries. The availability of vast supplies of arms encourages countries to try to solve their disagreements by war rather than by other means. The overall result is that the world is spending more and more on armaments each year without making the countries involved more secure.

Who has the bomb (and who owns up to having it)?

Yes
Countries that already 'officially' have their own nuclear weapons: USA, Soviet Union, France, Britain, China.

Maybe
Countries that may have nuclear weapons but don't admit to it: Israel, South Africa, India.

Nearly
Countries that could soon have nuclear weapons if they wanted to: Argentina, Brazil, Egypt, Iraq, Libya, Pakistan, South Korea, Taiwan.

The Chernobyl disaster, 1986

Many nuclear reactors not only produce electricity but also make plutonium for military use. Reactors can go disastrously wrong. In May 1986 the nuclear reactor at Chernobyl in the Soviet Union exploded and sent a poisonous cloud of radioactivity across not only Russia, but also parts of Scandinavia, Southern and Western Europe.

Millions of people were affected by the fallout. 135 000 people inhabiting an area of more than 56 sq km around the accident site had to abandon their homes. Water, livestock and food were contaminated even as far away as Britain. In parts of Cumbria, over a year after the accident, sheep had levels of radioactivity in their bodies so high that they could not be sold as food.

The long-term effects of the disaster are unknown but experts predict that, over the next twenty to thirty years, the fallout from Chernobyl is likely to lead to thousands of cancer deaths. The stricken reactor was eventually entombed beneath over 400 000 tonnes of cement: but the damage had already been done.

Nuclear proliferation

The term *nuclear proliferation* refers to the spread to an ever increasing number of countries of the knowledge and equipment needed to make nuclear bombs. In 1987 there were five major nuclear powers – countries that manufactured and held stocks of nuclear weapons and the systems needed to launch them: the USA, the Soviet Union, Britain, France and China. But the number of potential nuclear weapons states is bigger and growing. Many experts believe that Israel has secretly built several nuclear weapons. India exploded an underground nuclear 'device' in 1974. Pakistan is believed to have assembled all the equipment and parts it needs to make a number of nuclear bombs. In June 1981 the Israelis destroyed a nuclear reactor in Iraq which, they believed, was going to be used to manufacture plutonium for nuclear bombs. Some people believe that South Africa secretly exploded a test nuclear bomb in 1979. There is evidence that Argentina has been using its nuclear reactors to separate plutonium for possible use in nuclear weapons.

At the present time there are several countries on the verge of becoming nuclear-weapons states. Many more could have nuclear weapons within a few years if they wished to. It is possible that by the end of this century, about thirty countries, most of them in the Third World, could possess their own nuclear weapons. If this situation should come about, the chances of nuclear war occurring, possibly on a world-wide scale, will be much greater than they are now.

The fuel cycle and equipment transfers

As the fuel cycle diagram shows, there are two main routes to making nuclear weapons. One way is to enrich (or purify) natural uranium so that it is suitable for use in bombs. The other way is to put uranium into a nuclear reactor which, over a period of months, 'burns' the uranium. This process produces heat which can be used to generate electricity. As it 'burns' the uranium begins to turn into plutonium. This plutonium can later be retrieved in a reprocessing plant. It can then either be used in a reactor which 'burns' plutonium, or it can be used in a bomb.

For several years after 1945 the technology for using nuclear materials was a closely guarded secret which the Americans were not prepared to share even with their closest allies. Moreover the expense of building and operating nuclear plants for many years prevented all but the world's richest countries from developing a nuclear industry. But this has now all changed. By the end of 1984 there were 516 nuclear reactors in the world producing electricity. Nearly all of these are situated in more industrialised countries. However, there are twenty-nine Third World countries with small-scale research reactors (used to test various systems before installing a big power reactor). These can be used to create plutonium for bombs. This gives every country with a research reactor the opportunity of developing nuclear weapons. But, as the fuel cycle diagram shows, it is not possible to make nuclear weapons directly from uranium, or directly from nuclear reactors. What is needed to do this is either an *enrichment plant*, a supply of already-enriched uranium, or a plant to *reprocess* 'burned' uranium.

The nuclear fuel cycle

Nuclear weapons can be manufactured at two stages of the fuel cycle: after uranium enrichment, or by separating plutonium from used reactor fuel. It has been estimated that in 1984, 60 tonnes of plutonium was separated from spent fuel in the 54 countries with nuclear reactors. This was enough to make 7500 nuclear warheads. If only a fraction of this production were actually diverted to build warheads, it is easy to see how quickly the number of countries with nuclear weapons could grow.

The superpowers have been very reluctant to supply these plants to Third World countries because they have been concerned to prevent the proliferation of nuclear weapons. They have, however, been prepared to help build reactors, to train scientists and engineers, and to provide low-grade nuclear fuel for Third World countries as long as they agree not to try to make any bombs. But many countries have wanted at the least the ability to make nuclear weapons, perhaps for prestige reasons (what is good enough for the superpowers is good enough for us!) or perhaps as an insurance just in case an enemy should get hold of nuclear weapons. It has not been too difficult for countries such as India, Pakistan, Iraq and Argentina to get round the restrictions imposed by the superpowers. Moreover, countries like France, Germany, Switzerland and Italy, in an effort to make their own nuclear industries profitable, *have* been prepared to sell enrichment and reprocessing plants to various Third World countries. As a result several countries now have the means of making nuclear bombs if they wish to.

In 1968 a very important international treaty was signed. It was designed to prevent the spread of nuclear weapons beyond the existing 'nuclear club'. The treaty, known as the *Non-Proliferation Treaty* offered the countries that signed it every assistance in the development of nuclear energy for peaceful purposes as long as they

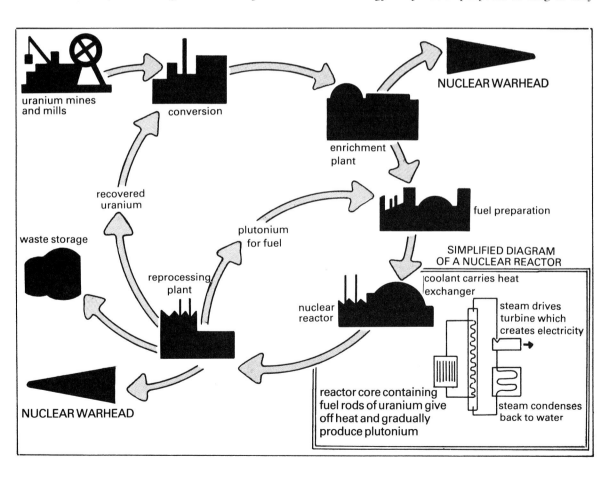

uranium mines and mills

conversion

NUCLEAR WARHEAD

enrichment plant

fuel preparation

recovered uranium

plutonium for fuel

SIMPLIFIED DIAGRAM OF A NUCLEAR REACTOR

waste storage

reprocessing plant

nuclear reactor

coolant carries heat exchanger

steam drives turbine which creates electricity

reactor core containing fuel rods of uranium give off heat and gradually produce plutonium

steam condenses back to water

NUCLEAR WARHEAD

Nuclear terrorism?

Although a very remote possibility, nuclear terrorism may be a possible result of the spread of nuclear know-how and supplies of plutonium to more and more countries. Terrorists have used bombing campaigns to put pressure on governments. What might they do if they had access to nuclear weapons, even of the crudest kind?

did not try to produce nuclear weapons. To keep a check on this the International Atomic Energy Agency was set up to try to ensure that no nuclear fuel intended for peaceful purposes could be diverted to the production of nuclear bombs. But there was no way of making every country sign this treaty. Many refused, saying that the treaty was only intended to allow the existing nuclear weapons countries to keep their weapons while denying them to others. The majority of countries now most likely to develop nuclear weapons did not sign the treaty. Even so they would find it very difficult to develop nuclear weapons if it were not so easy to buy the equipment they needed from Western companies anxious to sell it to them.

The spread of the ability to make nuclear weapons is a dangerous development. Many of the countries concerned, such as Israel, Taiwan and South Africa, feel that their very existence is threatened by hostile neighbours. It is possible that in a war with those neighbours, these countries would threaten to use or might actually employ nuclear weapons as a last resort. In some cases, countries that are trying to acquire nuclear weapons have been to war with each other several times already. Israel has been involved in several conflicts with its Arab neighbours over a period of many years, and so have Pakistan and India, and South Africa and surrounding countries.

As the existing weapons states had, by the mid 1980s, shown no signs at all of being willing to do without nuclear weapons, but rather have increased their dependence on them since the *Non-Proliferation Treaty* was signed, it is hardly surprising that many other countries see the possession of nuclear weapons as a symbol of security and power. If one country in a region of the world acquires nuclear weapons, its neighbours may not feel safe until they have them too.

The effects of the arms trade

The arms trade has helped many Third World governments to build up mighty military machines to crush internal opposition, to threaten neighbouring countries or to support wars for new territory. To that extent it has made the world a more dangerous and bloody place. It can be argued that where the superpowers are each arming opposing sides, there is a balance between them which helps to prevent war. But, as time passes, even where this is so, the balance operates at even higher levels of armaments. If the balance were ever to tip, that might be the signal for a long-awaited war.

One important reason for the willingness of the USA in particular to supply conventional weapons to countries like Israel, South Korea, Taiwan and Pakistan, has been an attempt to persuade them not to seek to develop nuclear weapons for themselves, but to rely on very strong conventional forces. But, as we have seen, countries such as France and Germany *have* been willing to supply equipment that could be used to make nuclear bombs. They have also been willing to supply weapons – such as fighters and bombers – which can be adapted to carry nuclear weapons. Thus, the conventional arms trade may perhaps have slowed down the dangerous process of nuclear proliferation (though there is little evidence of this) but it clearly has not put an end to it.

5 The dynamics of the arms race

The roots of the Cold War

Strategic nuclear weapons

In 1986 the USA possessed nearly 13 000 strategic nuclear warheads and the Russians had nearly 11 000. Three other countries possessed a few hundred warheads between them. This enormous arsenal, equal in destructive power to well over a million Hiroshima bombs, was built up in the space of only thirty-five years. Nuclear arms are the centre of the arms race between the superpowers even though they account for only about twenty per cent of all arms spending. In this chapter we explain how and why the nuclear arms race has occurred.

In 1939, just before the outbreak of the Second World War, Albert Einstein, the nuclear physicist, wrote an urgent letter to the President of the United States. It went as follows:

> *Some recent work...leads me to expect that the element uranium may be turned into a new and important source of energy in the immediate future...I believe...that extremely powerful bombs of a new type may...be constructed. I understand that Germany has actually stopped the sale of uranium from the Czechoslovakian mines which she has taken over.*

Einstein's letter alerted the United States and its allies to the possibility that Hitler might be trying to make atomic bombs. This persuaded the Americans, with the help of British scientists, to undertake secret work to produce bombs of their own. The work began in 1941. However, by 1945 it had become clear that Germany had never seriously tried to make an atomic bomb. Despite this, work went on, and after one small test, the first two atomic bombs were dropped on Japan. Within days of the second atomic explosion (over the city of Nagasaki) the Japanese surrendered. Many people hailed this as a justification for using the bomb – saving the thousands of lives that would have been lost in an invasion of Japan. But some others suggested that the main reason was to end the war in the East before the Russians entered it and began to claim their share of the spoils.

At this point some of those working on the development of America's bomb wanted to stop. They realised that once the atomic bomb had been used against people, the world could never be the same again, and the spread and eventual large-scale use of such weapons might not be prevented. But other opinions were to prevail.

Superpower hostility

Though the Americans and Russians had been allies during the Second World War, united against their common enemy, Germany,

FINAL EDITION

The All
🏴 American Times 🏴

vol. LXIV　　　　　AMERICA - APRIL 20, 1983 - SIXTEEN PAGES　　　　　cc ·　　no. 134

THE US VIEW OF THE WORLD

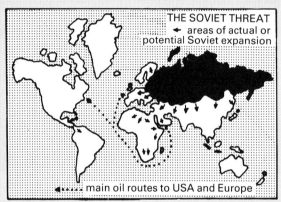

THE SOVIET THREAT
← areas of actual or potential Soviet expansion

◄····· main oil routes to USA and Europe

It is our belief that, since the communist revolution in Russia in 1917, the free countries of the world have been under threat from the Soviet Union, the declared enemy of all free nations. The Soviets are not a free society and they do not allow free institutions to exist wherever they are in control. Since the 1930s the Russians have singlemindedly set out to become the mightiest power on earth in order to achieve world domination. Since the end of the Second World War the Soviets have used every opportunity open to them to expand their power and influence. They have used their massive military forces to place other countries under their control from East Germany to Afghanistan. They have aided Communist revolutionaries in all parts of the world – in Africa, in South East Asia especially in Vietnam, in Cuba and recently in El Salvador and Nicaragua. They are prepared to exploit any crisis in any country to increase their power and influence.

Unless the Soviets are prepared to change their ways, we Americans have no choice but to lead the free world in opposition to them. No other country has the power or military strength to stand up to the Soviet Union so we must. We must challenge their efforts to undermine free governments and we must strive to contain communism within its present boundaries.

This does not mean that we want war with the Soviet Union. We know how disastrous a nuclear war could be. But there are certain things worth fighting for. We will defend our interests in every part of the world including the vulnerable sources of our oil, our life blood. We will resist any aggression by the Soviet Union on any of our allies. But at the same time we remain willing to talk peace and co-operation. We are willing to limit armaments and to reduce the levels of nuclear weapons. We have them to defend ourselves; to prevent aggression against us and our allies. If the Soviet Union will only reduce its military forces, ours would no longer be needed.

But if the Soviet Union continues to build up its forces as it has done without a halt for the last two decades, what else can we do? The Soviets have caught up with us in missile strength and now have a lead over us. They have more ships, more submarines, more soldiers, more guns, more tanks, more aircraft than we do. If we are to be firm and strong in our determination to resist the threat of Soviet expansion then we must remain militarily strong. And if the Soviets continue to modernise their forces, then so must we. If the Soviet Union really wants peace as it always says it does, then why does it spend more than any other nation on earth on weapons, and why has it increased its armaments well beyond any realistic level needed for defence? When we see reductions in Soviet arms, and withdrawal of their troops from foreign lands, then we will begin to believe that the Soviet Union is willing to live at peace with the rest of the world. Then we will reduce our own arms spending and military involvement abroad.

Soviet military interventions:

1945–47 East Germany,
　　　　　Poland,
　　　　　Czechoslovakia,
　　　　　Hungary,
　　　　　Rumania,
　　　　　Bulgaria

1948 Berlin

1956 Hungary

1960 Cuba

1968 Czechoslovakia

1970 Egypt

1974 Mozambique

1975 Angola

1978 Ethiopia

1979 Afghanistan

ВСЕСОЮЗНАЯ ПРАВДА

CCCP – 20 APRIL, 1983   FINAL EDITION   vol. LXVII   no. 561

THE SOVIET VIEW OF THE WORLD

The Americans are hypocrites when they accuse us of aggression. The Americans and their friends began their aggression many centuries ago when they colonised and exploited most parts of the world and grew fat on the proceeds. The capitalists believe they own the whole world. When a country emerges which challenges their domination their only reaction is to try to destroy it. Why else did American, British and French troops invade Russia only months after our revolution in 1917? Why else have they surrounded us with military bases and hostile military alliances? If they mean peace

US military interventions	
1950	South Korea
1950–70	Taiwan
1961	Cuba
1961–72	North and South Vietnam
1961–75	Laos
1963	Guyana
1965	Dominican Republic
1969–70	Thailand
1973	Chile
1970–75	Cambodia
1971–78	Zaire
1980	El Salvador
1981	Nicaragua

THE ENCIRCLEMENT OF THE SOVIET UNION

they have a strange way of showing it. The Americans say we are out to dominate the world by force. We do not need to. Capitalism will eventually destroy itself because it is a corrupt and illogical system, and all the people of the world will one day enjoy socialism. But, until that day comes, and as long as we have to face highly armed hostile countries around us then we must build up our strength to defend ourselves.

Our great leaders in the past said that if we were weak we would be destroyed. If we were strong we would survive. And so we wish to be strong. It is our strength that saves us and keeps our enemies at bay. But it is not enough for us just to sit behind our borders quietly while the Americans and other capitalists gobble up the world. We have to help our friends in other parts of the world who are fighting oppression and dictatorships. We have to show the West that, whatever the cost, they cannot strangle or surround us. We shall not take second place and will match every increase in armaments that the West makes. We do not want to dominate the world, we want to be secure and safe. But we believe that in a world of arms and war we must be as strong as possible.

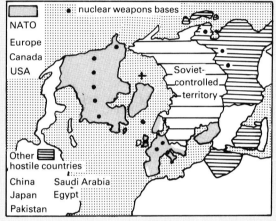

That does not mean that we want war. We do not. We mean it when we say we want peace. We know what it is like to suffer invasion and millions of deaths. The Americans do not. We have been invaded three times this century. It will not happen again. The Americans and their allies have dominated the world while we were weak. They can no longer do this. That is why they make such a fuss about Soviet military might. Yes, we are strong and we need to be. Remember that it is the Americans who have led every stage of the arms race. Who first developed the atom bomb? Which is the only country ever to have used it? Who introduced nuclear weapons into Europe? Who surrounds us with nuclear weapons? Who first supplied weapons

to Third World countries? Who first sent masses of troops to foreign countries to try to defeat those fighting for freedom? Not us. The Americans say that they believe in freedom and yet their money or soldiers have been used to overthrow democratic governments (for example in Chile and the Dominican Republic) and to support evil dictators who torture and starve their people (for example in Vietnam and El Salvador). The Americans say they believe in peace and yet use force to gain their objectives. In the face of this aggression the Russian people cannot afford to reduce their defences. We do not want war, and we will never start one. But if one is brought upon us by others we shall fight with all our strength, and we shall win.

there was, deep down, very little trust between the two superpowers. The Americans feared the influence of communism, and were desperately worried that it might spread like a forest fire through the world after the end of the war. The Soviet Union, as the first, largest and the most powerful communist state was therefore to be feared. The Americans believed that the Russians would try to expand their influence throughout the world and would try to overthrow or weaken capitalism wherever they could. For example, a secret report prepared for the American government in 1950 stated that the Russians were seeking:

> ... the complete overturning and destruction of the governments and the societies in the non-communist world and their replacement by a system and structure controlled from Moscow. The United States as the main centre of power outside the Soviet world and the main obstacle to Soviet expansion, is the main enemy who must be undermined or destroyed by one means or another.

The Russians, not surprisingly, had a different view of things. They were very worried about the new bomb which the Americans had developed. Their territory had already been invaded four times in recent history: by Japan in 1904, by Germany in 1914 and again in 1941, and by British, French, American and Canadian forces in 1917. Stalin, the Russian leader from 1924 to 1953, did not believe that the capitalist countries of the West really wanted peace with the Soviet Union. He probably believed that communism would eventually triumph over capitalism but that, until that day came, the strongest capitalist countries would do all in their power to crush the Soviet Union completely. In 1931 Stalin said:

> We do not want to be beaten... Russia... was ceaselessly beaten for her backwardness... We are fifty or a hundred years behind the advanced countries. We must make good this lag in ten years. Either we do it or they crush us.

One of Stalin's main aims was to make the Soviet Union a mighty economic and military power. In 1945 he believed that the USSR had only been able to defeat Hitler's invasion because it had put so much effort into building up its military and economic strength. Even so, at least 20 million Russian lives had been lost in the war and Stalin was determined that in future the Soviet Union must be so strong that no country would dare attack. It was this kind of thinking that lay behind the decision to invade and hold on to a belt of countries in Eastern Europe to act as a 'buffer' against invasion from the West. Also, the fear of being destroyed by enemies both outside and inside the country led Stalin to continue the build-up of Soviet military strength. Such forces could be used to counter attacks from outside, or subversion from within the Soviet Union or Eastern Europe. Stalin was therefore determined at all costs to keep pace with the Western nations and to hide what was going on in the Soviet Union from the eyes of the outside world. In particular the Russians were determined that they too should have the atom bomb.

The fears and mistrust between the two superpowers provide the background to the nuclear arms race and are among the main obstacles to attempts to halt its progress.

Early efforts to control nuclear weapons

After the war several attempts were made to control the development of nuclear technology and to prevent a nuclear arms race. All were to fail. The Russians were, as we have seen, very suspicious of the USA having the atomic bomb while they did not. The Americans hoped to prevent the Soviet Union from getting the bomb by getting it to agree to put nuclear weapons under international control. But if the Russians could not be brought to agree to this, the Americans were determined to keep well ahead in the number and quality of nuclear weaponry.

In 1946 the Americans proposed that nuclear energy should come under international control through the newly established United Nations. Under the terms of the proposal an international agency would control the world's nuclear energy for peaceful purposes and all nuclear weapons would be banned. Every country would have to open its military facilities to inspectors from the international agency who would check that they were not secretly building or stock-piling nuclear weapons. The Russians rejected the plan saying that the proposed agency would not be neutral but would be under US control, so that the agency's inspectors would be little more than spies looking out for Soviet weak spots. The Russians wanted the Americans to give up their nuclear weapons *first*, and then work out a treaty to control nuclear energy. This idea was unacceptable to the Americans who went on producing and testing nuclear weapons while these talks were going on. American military leaders were worried that, if the USA got rid of its own nuclear weapons first, the Russians might secretly develop their own or might use their superior conventional forces to extend Soviet control over more countries.

In fact, the Russians had already been working hard to produce their own atomic bomb. When they tested it in 1949 this only confirmed America's worst suspicions. As the Cold War intensified

The Bikini test, 1954

The Americans continued to develop and test nuclear weapons of various kinds even while engaged in discussions with the Russians to ban them. The US Army and Air Forces seemed very keen to demonstrate their new weapons. The photograph shows the explosion of a US hydrogen bomb at Bikini Atoll in the Pacific.

the Americans went into full-scale production of nuclear weapons. The nuclear arms race had begun.

The failure of these early attempts reflected the atmosphere of fear and mistrust that existed then and later between the two superpowers. Any treaty that was to be acceptable to both sides had to guarantee the security of both sides and had to make 'cheating' impossible. In the climate of the Cold War such an agreement only once seemed close. But if it was impossible to reach an agreement in the 1940s when there were only a few simple bombs around, and for much of this time in the hands of only one country, how much more daunting has the task become in later years. The number and types of weapons have increased massively, and more and more countries are now involved.

The military–industrial complex

The military–industrial complex

As the arms race has gathered pace, both superpowers have developed massive organisations to produce, supply and operate their weapons systems. If we add together the people who design and manufacture the weapons, those who supply them and those who use them, then this adds up to an enormous number of people who

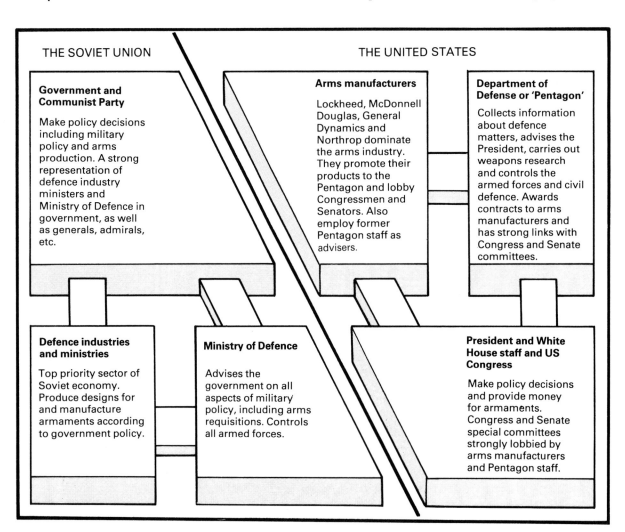

THE SOVIET UNION

THE UNITED STATES

Government and Communist Party

Make policy decisions including military policy and arms production. A strong representation of defence industry ministers and Ministry of Defence in government, as well as generals, admirals, etc.

Arms manufacturers

Lockheed, McDonnell Douglas, General Dynamics and Northrop dominate the arms industry. They promote their products to the Pentagon and lobby Congressmen and Senators. Also employ former Pentagon staff as advisers.

Department of Defense or 'Pentagon'

Collects information about defence matters, advises the President, carries out weapons research and controls the armed forces and civil defence. Awards contracts to arms manufacturers and has strong links with Congress and Senate committees.

Defence industries and ministries

Top priority sector of Soviet economy. Produce designs for and manufacture armaments according to government policy.

Ministry of Defence

Advises the government on all aspects of military policy, including arms requisitions. Controls all armed forces.

President and White House staff and US Congress

Make policy decisions and provide money for armaments. Congress and Senate special committees strongly lobbied by arms manufacturers and Pentagon staff.

are, in one way or another, dependent upon the arms race for a living. For these people the arms race means jobs, security and money, and for some of them, considerable political power too. For those at the top of these organisations (the generals, admirals, leading research scientists and engineers and the managers of manufacturing companies) the production of more and better weapons is a way in which they can directly contribute towards what they believe is the security of their country. But it also obtains for them well-paid and influential jobs in their society. As a group, these people have considerable influence over political leaders – pushing for new weapons, warning of weaknesses in the existing defences, and alerting people to the strengths of the enemy. This grouping, usually known as the *military–industrial complex*, operates in both the Soviet Union and the USA, though in different ways in each country.

In the Soviet Union, leading military figures are at the very centre of political power. Their close involvement in government decisions reflects the great importance that the Soviet leaders have always given to military strength, which is regarded as absolutely essential to the survival of the communist system in the Soviet Union and of the country itself. Military spending and military service are highly valued. All men have to do military service. There is compulsory 'military-patriotic' education in schools. The production of military equipment is given top priority and has access to top-quality materials and workers when the rest of the economy may suffer from poor quality and shortage of resources. The Russian people are told that they must make sacrifices in order to pay for the armed forces and weapons needed to ensure peace and to prevent aggression against them.

In the Soviet Union therefore, the top political leaders, the high military men and those in charge of the ministries which produce the hardware are all brought together. What goes on in these circles we cannot know, for the Soviet Union is a closed and secretive society. However, we can guess that the political leaders look to their military leaders for advice on defence. These military leaders will naturally want the best possible equipment and resources, and these desires will provide work and responsibilities for the ministries which are in charge of military production. Because of their position in Soviet society, it is only to be expected that the military and industrial groups will press for more resources and will point out weaknesses that must be put right by spending more on weapons. What eventually happens will depend on the balance of opinions among the political leaders, many of whom have military backgrounds. In the Soviet Union there is a strong tendency to try to resolve problems by using force. Convinced as they are that military strength saved them from defeat in the Second World War and saves them from attack now, there are strong pressures to build up arms even more.

In the United States the military–industrial complex has been nicknamed the *iron triangle* because it is made up of three main groups. One corner is filled by the arms manufacturing companies, another by the armed forces and defence ministries which use those arms. (The people who control this second group are housed together in a building known as the Pentagon.) Finally there is Congress (the US parliament) which provides money for the development and production of the weapons. There are close links between all three corners of the iron triangle. The weapons

US arms manufacturers are keen to recruit the best talent available to design and build new weapons systems. This advertisement for recruits came from *Aviation Week and Space Technology*, June 1985

manufacturers need to make profits; so they need orders for weapons. The main source of orders is the government; and the government decides what to order according to what it thinks is necessary. This is where the Pentagon comes in. The military advisers and planners in the Pentagon award research contracts to scientists and engineers. They also decide what weapons they think the country needs and try to persuade Congress and the government to buy them.

Since big government contracts can make all the difference to the profits of companies they push their products very hard. If they are successful this means secure profits and more jobs. If they fail it could mean that thousands of men and women would be sacked. Therefore the companies and trade unions send out teams of people to try to persuade Congressmen, Senators and Pentagon planners of the need for this or that weapons system. Most companies frequently come up with new systems for which greater efficiency, destructive power or accuracy is claimed. They sometimes also undertake studies of Soviet strengths to back up their case for the need to buy the aircraft or missiles they are offering for sale. The US military–industrial complex is made up of a body of people whose power, influence and livelihoods depend upon the arms race. They keep up a constant pressure for increased arms spending. The research laboratories of the weapons manufacturing companies and of the Pentagon's own weapons research agency are continually coming up with new and 'better' weapons. These obviously appeal to planners and military leaders who want the best available. Many of the Star Wars weapons systems were developed and promoted in this way.

This does not mean that politicians are unable to cut down on arms expenditure. Several US Presidents have cancelled projects and cut arms spending. In 1977, for example, President Carter cancelled the B-1 bomber project. It is difficult to know what happens behind the closed doors of the Kremlin. Even the total spending on armaments in the Soviet Union is a matter of guesswork, though it appears that Soviet spending on weapons has constantly risen. What is clear is that the arms lobbies (arms industries, the military forces and politicians linked to them) are strong and well organised in *both* superpowers. In a very real sense the military–industrial complex in each superpower feeds off the other: fear of the other's capabilities and intentions leads to pressure for new weapons and more spending. This in turn creates fear on the other side and similar pressures for a further build-up. In these ways the superpowers have become locked into an upward spiral of arms spending and new weapons technology. In the next section we look at two examples of this process.

Missiles and warheads

ICBM stands for intercontinental ballistic missile. This is a missile based on land which can reach the Soviet Union from the USA or vice versa.

SLBM stands for submarine-launched ballistic missile. This is a ballistic missile carried in or launched from a submarine.

ABM stands for anti-ballistic missile. This is a system designed to intercept and shoot down an incoming nuclear warhead. It is the only existing form of active defence against nuclear attack and can easily be smothered by the large number of incoming warheads. At present it consists of very fast ballistic missiles; however, lasers or particle beams may form the ABM systems of the future.

MIRV stands for multiple independently targetable re-entry vehicle. This is a re-entry vehicle launched by a ballistic missile which can carry several warheads, each of which can be guided to a different target.

The 'missile gap'

In the early years of the nuclear arms race the Americans were certain that they were well ahead of the Russians. They had more warheads and more aircraft to deliver them: 600 compared to the Soviet Union's 200. They were therefore deeply shocked when, in 1957, the Russians placed the world's first satellite into orbit around the earth. The *Sputnik* launch seemed to indicate that the Russians had mastered advanced electronic and rocket technology. Both superpowers were at that time experimenting with putting nuclear warheads on top of rockets which would cut the time taken to deliver warheads to their target from several hours to about thirty minutes. This development would also make it harder to shoot the warheads down. The Americans began to think that perhaps the Russians were ahead in this respect, and began to fear that their nuclear bomber forces would soon become vulnerable to a surprise Soviet attack.

Their fears were increased by photographs which were brought back by high-flying spy planes (such as the U-2) which seemed to show that the Russians were building missile silos. American defence experts were not sure how many silos there were, nor how many the Russians planned to build. Many politicians and military planners began to argue that the government was neglecting US defences. Reports from the US Air Force (in charge of America's missiles) suggested that the Russians would have 100 missiles in place by 1960 while America would have only 30. The Russians would, the report said, add 500 a year from then on so that by 1964, they would have 2000 compared to the Americans' 130. Although not everyone accepted these figures, many Pentagon experts believed that the Russians would have 500 missiles in place by 1961 and so urged a massive build-up of US missiles to counter this expected Soviet threat.

The Americans therefore decided on a large increase in their nuclear forces over the next few years: producing over 1000 land-based missiles and starting a programme to build over 600 missiles that could be launched from submarines. It was not long before fresh evidence appeared which showed that the earlier estimates of Soviet strength and intentions were incorrect. In 1961 the Russians had in fact only four *intercontinental ballistic missiles* (*ICBMs*), not 500. By 1963 they had built 100, not the 1500 the USAF had predicted. Nevertheless, the US missile expansion programme went ahead and so by the mid 1960s gave the Americans a considerable nuclear superiority over the Russians.

This must have alarmed the Soviet Union. We do not know how many missiles they had originally planned to build but it is now clear that, from 1965, they too began to increase greatly their missile strength and began to put nuclear missiles in submarines. By

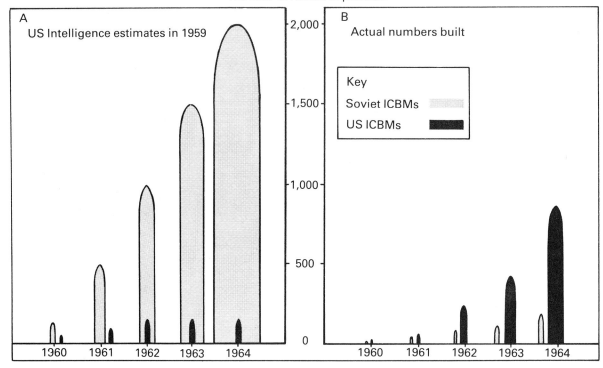

Number of ICBMs in position

A
US Intelligence estimates in 1959

B
Actual numbers built

Key
Soviet ICBMs
US ICBMs

The missile gap

US intelligence agencies predicted a massive lead for the Soviet Union in missiles (diagram A). In fact, the Russians only planned to produce a small number and the Americans soon overtook them (diagram B).

the late 1960s the arms race had reached a new high level. Both superpowers were about level with land-based missiles while the Russians were beginning to catch up with their submarine-launched missiles. But by this date there were many voices in the USA arguing once again that US defences were not strong enough in the face of the mounting Soviet threat.

The 'ABM gap' and MIRVs

During the 1960s the USA put into orbit a number of spy satellites to photograph the Soviet Union from space. The detail on these pictures was clear enough for the Americans to have a good idea about what the Russians were doing. Towards the end of the decade they revealed that the Russians were building large air-defence systems, at first around Moscow and later elsewhere. Some American experts argued that these defences could be used to shoot down incoming missiles. If they could do this the US defence experts believed that the Minuteman force could not be sure of reaching its targets. The Americans would no longer have a means of retaliation against a Soviet attack.

The Pentagon argued that the USA should overcome this problem by fitting their missiles with multiple warheads which would increase the chances of getting through Soviet defences. Some US experts also believed that the Russians had already tested their own multiple warheads and argued that unless the USA pressed ahead quickly with a *multiple independently targetable re-entry vehicle (MIRV)* programme for its missiles, it would fall behind the Russians who would have more warheads in any nuclear exchange. The US government therefore decided to 'MIRV' most of its missiles, thereby

A Soviet ship leaving Cuba. The missiles can clearly be seen on its decks. If the Soviet Union had succeeded in placing nuclear missiles in Cuba it would have acquired a similar ability to threaten the USA, as the United States already had in its nuclear bases in Europe, which threatened the Soviet Union from very close quarters.

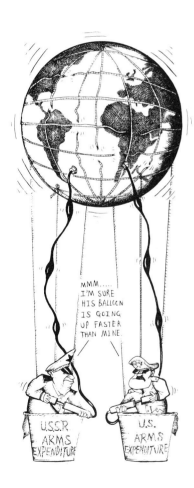

MMM..... I'M SURE HIS BALLOON IS GOING UP FASTER THAN MINE.

U.S.S.R. ARMS EXPENDITURE

U.S. ARMS EXPENDITURE

adding a strong new upward pressure to the nuclear arms race. Between 1968 and 1973 the USA more than doubled the number of warheads on long-range missiles (from 2270 to 5210). This meant that the US missiles could now hit a much larger number of Soviet targets. The new warheads were much more accurate too.

By 1973, however, the USA and Soviet Union had agreed not to develop large *anti-ballistic missile (ABM)* systems. And by then it had become clear that the Russians did not have any MIRVed warheads at all. But the Russians were determined not to be outdone by the USA and embarked upon a programme to MIRV their missiles in 1975. As a result the number of warheads carried by Soviet long-range missiles rose from 2308 in 1975 to 6848 in 1981. By this date the number of US warheads had reached 7032.

Some people argue that examples such as these show that the USA has been largely responsible for speeding up the nuclear arms race. They argue that there is a strong tendency for the US military–industrial complex to put forward the '*worst-case*' picture of the future. This means, they argue, that US defences should more than match the worst that the Russians could conceivably do at some date in the future. They not only frequently exaggerate what the Russians are capable of doing, but appear to assume that the Russians actually want to do the most that they are capable of. They are not impressed by the argument that most Soviet developments in nuclear weapons have been efforts to catch up and gain equality with the Americans. Critics of the American military–industrial complex argue that in the USA new weapons are introduced not because there is a real need for them but because the manufacturers want contracts, the politicians want jobs for their voters, and each branch of the armed forces wants better and more up-to-date equipment than the others have. When one particular 'gap' has been closed or shown to be unimportant, a new one emerges to take its place. Thus, it is argued, American attitudes to the arms race tend to reflect American needs rather than Russian threats.

There is certainly some truth in this, but the Russians have also been partly to blame for creating this American attitude. They have always been extremely secretive about their military plans, and they have in the past acted aggressively in Berlin and Korea and more recently in Afghanistan. In earlier years they too boasted about the strength of their nuclear weapons. This has understandably

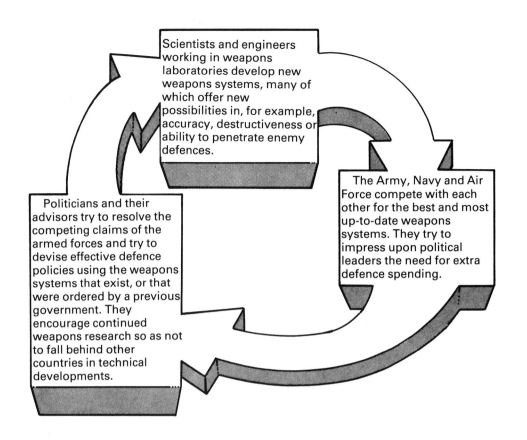

Scientists and engineers working in weapons laboratories develop new weapons systems, many of which offer new possibilities in, for example, accuracy, destructiveness or ability to penetrate enemy defences.

The Army, Navy and Air Force compete with each other for the best and most up-to-date weapons systems. They try to impress upon political leaders the need for extra defence spending.

Politicians and their advisors try to resolve the competing claims of the armed forces and try to devise effective defence policies using the weapons systems that exist, or that were ordered by a previous government. They encourage continued weapons research so as not to fall behind other countries in technical developments.

Technological improvements are an important feature of the arms race. Scientists and engineers in both superpowers and their allies are constantly devising and developing new systems. Research on a weapon system begins many years before there might be any military need for it; but the research is often justified by the need to keep ahead of the other side in case they too are working on similar lines. Once a new system becomes available, it is hard to resist deploying it.

encouraged American fears and has given more weight to the 'pessimists' in the US military–industrial complex. It has also given great influence to US intelligence agencies whose guesses about Soviet strength and capabilities have often been inaccurate and exaggerated. US governments have therefore tended to fear the worst and to plan accordingly.

. Since the 1960s the Soviet Union has managed to close the gap with the United States in nuclear weapons and has modernised and increased the size of all its armed forces, particularly its navy. In the 1970s the Americans hoped that, once the Russians had caught up, the two superpowers could agree to an upper limit to their nuclear forces. The Russians have said that they will only feel secure once they regard their forces and those of the USA to be broadly in balance. However, they were only able to reach very limited agreement which did little to restrict the arms build-up.

By the early 1980s the Russians were declaring that there now existed a rough nuclear balance between the two superpowers so that both could begin to consider real balanced reductions in their forces. But the Americans had been both surprised by the sophistication of new Soviet missiles and alarmed by the speed at which they had caught up. Many voices were raised in the USA arguing that US defences had been allowed to run down while the Soviet Union raced ahead, particularly in developing more accurate missiles. Accordingly, when Ronald Reagan was elected US President in 1980 on a promise to restore American defences to an adequate level, he proposed the largest weapons build-up the USA had ever witnessed in peacetime.

As a result the USA embarked upon a massive modernisation programme for all branches of its armed forces. This programme involves fitting 1500 cruise missiles to B-52 bombers and 4000 cruise missiles to surface ships and submarines. One hundred new supersonic nuclear B-1B bombers are being built, as well as up to twenty-five Trident submarines, each armed with twenty-four missiles, and each missile carrying eight highly accurate warheads. Two new ICBMS – the large MX and the single-warhead Midgetman – are planned. By the 1990s the USA will possess modern nuclear forces which can deliver nuclear warheads very accurately from land, sea or air. The modernisation programme, when added to Star Wars research has meant a lot of work and large profits for the major US arms manufacturing companies.

For their part, the Russians are reported to be modernising seventeen nuclear systems and to be undertaking their own ballistic missile defence programme. In the absence of any negotiated arms control treaty they have threatened to match all developments made by the USA. Most analysts, however, estimate that the Soviet Union lags behind the USA in electronics, miniaturisation and computer-control. From the evidence of the past, however, it is to be expected that the Russians will catch up faster than expected.

The MX missile

In 1986 the first of a hundred MX ICBMs was deployed. Each MX can deliver 10–12 independently targetable warheads over a range of 13 000 km to within 130 m of their targets. The photograph shows dummy warheads being fitted to an MX 'bus' platform.

6 The changing face of deterrence

The last minutes of peace

The red telephone beside the President's bed bleeped urgently. As his sleep drifted away from him, his Secretary of State and several military aides rushed in. The nightmare had begun.

'The Israelis have struck Damascus and Baghdad with nuclear weapons. Soviet and US naval forces are in combat in the Indian Ocean and Mediterranean.'

Tense voices at his side as he was almost pushed into an overcoat, down the long staircase and out onto the back lawn where a helicopter, its rotor blades spinning, was already waiting. In the ten minutes it took to get to Andrews Air Force base, he was told of the events of the night and of the fears that the Russians would intervene to defend their allies. He knew that the final decisions had to be his. As Commander-in-Chief of all US Forces, his was the only voice that could send them off to war. He knew. He had been briefed. But his mind was as numb as death.

'My family?...' was all he could say.

'Safe. In a bunker at Fort Ritchie by now,' came the reply.

Out of the helicopter and running across the tarmac. Up the steps into the Boeing E-4B, the National Emergency Airborne Command Centre. As he entered, the coolness of the air conditioning and the hum of voices at control panels and shapes on displays jarred him into the realisation that this time it was for real. As the aircraft smoothly climbed towards its operational height of 10 000 metres, he felt the panic rise in his throat. The calm, practised voices of his advisers and the heads of the armed forces did little to calm him. He could not take it all in. Around the world, US forces were at the highest level of alert. Bomber pilots in Europe were ready to scramble. The big B-52s were already in the air. The submarines would only take 15 minutes to launch their missiles on command from him. The land-based missiles would take even less time.

They were in direct link with Strategic Air Command HQ in Nebraska. The Boeing jet could stay aloft for three days. Its crew and commanders could watch and control the entire war from their perch. The aircraft was insulated against the heat of nuclear blasts. The occupants would not experience the war outside.

'Emergency Action Message from SAC HQ, sir!' Heads turned towards the colonel who was in constant contact with Nebraska. 'First satellite reports indicate rocket ignitions over Eastern Russia.' 'Surely it is a mistake? They could not be trying to pre-empt, surely not! There are plenty of other options open. Ask for a check. Try the hot-line.' The President fought his desire to retch. Now above all he must think clearly.

'Fylingdales, England, sir. They confirm missile launches. Estimated time of arrival, 03.28. That is 20 minutes from now, sir. Confidence high that they are aimed at Minuteman bases.'

Another voice. 'Telex, sir, from Moscow. "The President is not available at the moment. Please hold".'

He was led away from the battle deck into the comfortable surroundings of the conference room.

'You have a number of options, sir, and about 3 minutes to decide. They are as follows: you could hold all forces until the attack arrives and then retaliate with what is left. You could order a full Minuteman launch immediately, or you could exercise the full targeting option employing all our forces. The decision is yours, sir!'

This could be what the last few minutes of peace on earth might be like if deterrence breaks down, though it is increasingly likely that the first move in nuclear war would be to knock out all of the enemy's command and control satellite links. If that happened, even the few minutes of calculated reaction in our example would be impossible.

The example we have used depicts the scene in the USA. It might have been set in Moscow. It is the nightmare that lies behind nuclear deterrence. If deterrence works, the nightmare will never be acted out. In this chapter we look at the idea of deterrence, and how it has changed over the last thirty-five years or so. This involves looking at the plans that have been made for the use of nuclear weapons in warfare.

An E-4B national emergency airborne command post

The US Air Force operates several national emergency airborne command posts. From any one of these aircraft the US President and top military men could control and direct a nuclear war. Not only can communications be sent to nuclear submarines, air bases and naval fleets across the globe but, if necessary, the 1000 Minuteman strategic missiles scattered around various bases in the USA could be fired by direct command from this aircraft, nicknamed the 'kneecap'.

Why have a nuclear deterrent?

Because of the particularly horrific nature of nuclear war, political leaders have rarely argued that they would use nuclear weapons to achieve their goals, unless such weapons were used against them first, or unless they were on the verge of defeat in a conventional war. Instead, they have employed the world *deterrence* to justify their country's possession of nuclear weapons. The idea of deterrence is to prevent an attack by threatening to retaliate so hard that what the attacker would suffer would outweigh any gains it may have hoped to make. For example, the fear of being caught and punished deters

most people from committing crimes, provided that the punishment is severe enough. Nuclear deterrence works in a similar way. The whole point of nuclear deterrence is that the very fear of nuclear war will prevent major acts of aggression, because no country would behave in such a way as to invite nuclear retaliation. No aggression could be worth the total destruction of one's own country with cities and industries wiped out and most of one's people dead. Since no way has yet been found to defend a country against nuclear weapons (after all it only needs one to get through to destroy a country's capital city), in theory at least, any country which has a nuclear deterrent need never again fear serious aggression from another country. No enemy could ever gain more than it risked losing in an attack.

Mutual assured destruction (MAD)

It is widely asserted that nuclear weapons have prevented war between the superpowers since the 1950s. For a few years after the end of the Second World War the Americans had a monopoly of nuclear weapons. Their policy was, during those early years, to threaten to use them against communist aggression anywhere in the world, and there were some American generals who later suggested using nuclear weapons against North Korea during the Korean War. However, no such use of nuclear weapons was ever made and within the space of a few years the Russians had developed nuclear weapons of their own.

By the early 1960s, both superpowers possessed enough nuclear warheads to deliver terrible destruction upon the cities and populations of one another. This situation became known as *mutual assured destruction*, or MAD for short. The key to MAD was the ability of either side to strike back or retaliate even after having been hit by a surprise attack from the other. In the 1960s, the weapons available to the superpowers were not very accurate. Therefore neither side could be certain of being able to destroy even a sizeable proportion of the other's nuclear forces in a surprise attack. Hence there was no conceivable situation in which it would ever be sensible for one superpower to attack the other, because it was certain that the other would have enough weapons left after a surprise attack to destroy the cities and industries of the attacker. Deterrence seemed to work because it was clear that the country that launched a nuclear attack would be bringing about its own destruction. Thus a third world war could be avoided and peace preserved through the maintenance of nuclear deterrence.

If both sides, with the weapons at their disposal in the early 1960s, were at that time able to destroy each other's cities, why did matters not stop there? Why did they add to the numbers of weapons they held? Why did they begin to build missile forces based both on land and in submarines? Why, in other words, did they think they needed thousands of nuclear warheads when hundreds would do the job? There are several possible answers to these questions.

Many military planners in both the USA and the Soviet Union were never really very happy with the idea of *minimum deterrence*: the idea that a country was safe if it had just enough weapons to wreak 'unacceptable' levels of destruction upon an enemy. One problem they had was how to be sure that their nuclear forces could, under every possible circumstance, reach their targets. The

Minimum deterrence

There are at most 200 cities in each superpower with more than 100 000 people. Assuming two warheads for each city, then a nuclear force of just 400 warheads on each side would be enough to maintain a credible nuclear deterrent based on the principles of MAD. Two Trident II submarines would be enough to do this. The US Navy plans to deploy 20–25 such submarines.

planners had to do what they could to protect their weapons from a surprise attack. For the Americans this meant nuclear bombers would not be adequate because they could be too easily destroyed on the ground, or shot down on the way to their targets. They decided that their nuclear deterrent should be based on three separate groups of weapons (known as the *triad*): missiles based in concrete silos, submarines hidden in the ocean depths and the original bomber forces. These were built up so that, even if the other two legs of the triad were destroyed by a surprise attack, the one remaining would still be enough to deliver the necessary destruction. The Russians too developed land-based missiles in the late 1950s, and submarines from the mid 1960s.

There was, however, another feature of the nuclear deterrent which military and political leaders were unhappy about. The problem that they saw in the idea of mutual assured destruction was that the deterrent only worked as long as one side believed that the other side would be prepared to use it. What if the enemy attacked with a limited strike, say against your bomber bases and missile forces? What should the response be? If you launched a full retaliation against the enemy's cities, then you would just be inviting

Changes in US nuclear strategy 1945–1980s

Late 1940s, early 1950s

Nuclear monopoly

No special role for nuclear weapons. The US had relatively few of them, the Russians only tested their first bomb in 1949.

Nuclear weapons were too new and hopes were still high that nuclear weapons could be banned by treaty. This discouraged the development of policies based on the threat to use them.

Mid–late 1950s

Massive retaliation

This was a policy of threatening to use nuclear weapons, possibly in massive numbers, to retaliate against communist agression anywhere in the world. Since the USA now possessed enough nuclear weapons to destroy the Soviet Union, this threat was designed to contain Soviet communism within the borders of those countries that were then communist. In this period deterrence was based on undisputed American nuclear superiority.

1960s–early 1970s

Mutual assured destruction

With increased numbers of weapons and delivery systems on both sides, each could be sure of being able to destroy the other. The important principle of MAD was the ability to do this even after having been hit by a surprise attack from the other side. In this period deterrence was based on the belief that neither side could hope to defeat the other by launching a nuclear attack.

Mid 1970s–1980s

Counterforce

Although not a new idea, counterforce strategy was encouraged by the growth in numbers of nuclear weapons and by their improved accuracy. The 'all-or-nothing' nature of MAD was felt to be too rigid. Counterforce was based on the idea of flexible retaliation, that is the ability to react to a nuclear attack with a range of possible responses from small to large scale, but essentially concentrating on the destruction of enemy weapons and military forces rather than cities and civilian population.

your own destruction. But if you did not do that, what could you do, other than surrender? Military and political leaders did not like the idea of the mutual assured destruction of each other's cities because it was too inflexible and it gave the initiative to the attacker. What is the point, they argued, in having weapons we dare not use?

From MAD to counterforce

During the 1960s, and possibly even earlier, both superpowers began to devise ways of using nuclear weapons more flexibly. The Russians appeared to regard nuclear deterrence as a threat to use nuclear weapons to fight and if possible win a nuclear war if ever they were attacked. In the USA there were increasing doubts about whether the strategy of MAD would actually work if it ever came to a crisis. Nuclear strategy therefore gradually shifted away from the idea of launching one massive retaliatory blow against the other side's cities and industries. Instead, plans were developed to use nuclear weapons in a variety of ways in response to different levels of aggression, ranging from small selective strikes against military targets (airports, missile sites, command centres, etc.) in response to limited aggression, right up to large-scale destruction of cities. This strategy, which became known as *counterforce*, emphasised the use of nuclear weapons in the first instance against the other side's military capabilities rather than against its civilian population.

Counterforce strategy developed and gained hold as technological developments emerged from the weapons laboratories which made it possible to believe that one might use nuclear weapons in a controlled and flexible way. Three conditions have to be met for a country to have a nuclear deterrent based upon a counterforce strategy. First, a large number of different kinds of nuclear weapons is needed to cover a wide range of different types of targets. Second, these weapons need to be accurately guided so that they can be very sure of hitting their targets. Third, it has to be possible to use nuclear weapons in a controlled and flexible way, making a selective use of force and responding quickly and effectively to changes in the war-fighting.

Thus the basis of nuclear deterrence based upon a counterforce strategy is the threat to respond to military aggression by hitting the attacker's military forces. It is argued that counterforce has the great advantage over MAD of being more credible (or believable) because it is able to cope with a whole range of aggression which falls short of an all-out attack on cities. Few people, however, believe that such a war would remain 'limited' for very long. There are great dangers that any use of nuclear weapons, even in a small way, would rapidly escalate to all-out nuclear war.

It is claimed that counterforce strategy is more believable and flexible than MAD and is therefore a better deterrent. But it also carries with it several new risks. One of the most notable features of counterforce strategy is that the weapons systems involved are more effective in an attacking role than in response to an attack. Whereas the strategy of MAD tended to favour the side that retaliated, counterforce favours the side that strikes first.

This is so for two main reasons. First, it is best to hit the other side before it can launch its weapons. Since there is no point in destroying empty missile silos, for example, or empty airports, the side that strikes second is at a great disadvantage. The second reason why it is better to strike first is the lack of time to make decisions

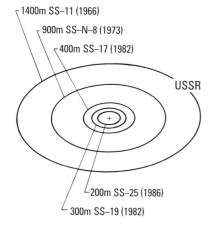

1400m SS–11 (1966)
900m SS–N–8 (1973)
400m SS–17 (1982)
USSR
200m SS–25 (1986)
300m SS–19 (1982)

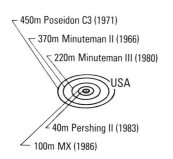

450m Poseidon C3 (1971)
370m Minuteman II (1966)
220m Minuteman III (1980)
USA
40m Pershing II (1983)
100m MX (1986)

Increasing accuracy of warheads

Earlier warheads were less accurate. This was adequate for the strategy of MAD. Considerable technological improvements in warhead design and missile guidance systems have yielded the accuracy required for a counterforce strategy. Although the Russians are behind the Americans, they are rapidly catching up.

Source: *IISS*

Strategic forces of the superpowers

Delivery systems and launchers of the superpowers in 1986

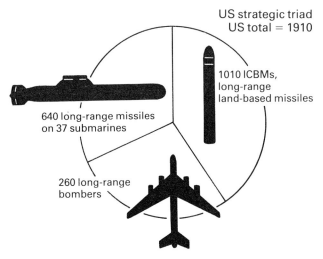

US strategic triad
US total = 1910

640 long-range missiles on 37 submarines

1010 ICBMs, long-range land-based missiles

260 long-range bombers

The long-range nuclear forces of the superpowers form the backbone of their deterrent. They are made up of three parts: long-range bombers, submarine-launched and land-based missiles. The forces of the USA are more evenly balanced than those of the Soviet Union which relies heavily on land-based missiles in fixed silos.

Soviet strategic forces
Soviet total = 2502

1398 ICBMs, long-range land-based missiles

160 long-range bombers

944 long-range missiles on 61 submarines

The Soviet Union has more ICBMs and missile-carrying submarines than the USA. However, many Soviet submarines are relatively noisy in operation and quite old, making them easier for the Americans to detect at sea. Moreover, because of technical problems, for example they have no harbours which are free from ice all year round, the Soviet Union usually has *fewer* submarines at sea than the USA. New Soviet submarines and more accurate missiles due to be introduced throughout the 1980s will, however, help to overcome many of these problems.

Is there a nuclear balance?

It is not possible to give a clear answer to this question. There are several ways of measuring the nuclear forces of the two superpowers and each measure gives different totals. The comparison of forces (left) shows that the Soviet Union is ahead of the USA in the number of launchers for missiles and bombs. But this way of measuring the forces conceals the fact that the USA generally has many more warheads on each missile and launcher than the Soviet Union. Also the Americans are well ahead of the Russians in fitting their long-range bomber fleet with accurate target-seeking missiles such as the cruise missile and the short-range attack missile. These can be launched from aircraft when they are a considerable distance from their targets.

If we compare warhead numbers we get impression one:

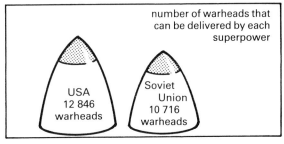

number of warheads that can be delivered by each superpower

USA 12 846 warheads

Soviet Union 10 716 warheads

But if we compare the superpowers' weapons in another way, the balance is once again reversed. On average, Soviet warheads are larger than US ones. Some experts argue that this more than makes up for the US lead in warheads, because larger warheads can create destruction over wider areas.

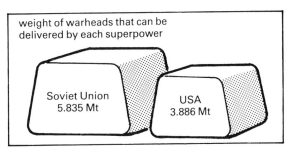

weight of warheads that can be delivered by each superpower

Soviet Union 5.835 Mt

USA 3.886 Mt

With so many different ways of measuring, there is clearly a great deal of room for disagreement among defence experts. Some people, however, argue that the forces held by both sides are so much greater than they need for deterrence that the idea of a strategic nuclear balance has no meaning. Just one submarine on either side is enough to destroy all the major cities of the other. However, in the 1980s both superpowers have continued to develop and deploy more new weapons systems.
Source: *IISS and SIPRI*

once under attack. While a country's leaders might receive thirty minutes' warning of an incoming ICBM attack, it might be less than ten minutes for a submarine attack. Clearly in such situations a planned and calculated response would be very difficult, especially if the attack began by destroying the other side's communications satellites.

The risks of counterforce

In a crisis, where tension has mounted between the superpowers and perhaps some conventional forces have already been in action, there will be considerable temptation to attack first. In other words, whereas deterrence under MAD was relatively stable because neither side could hope to gain victory by starting a nuclear war, counterforce strategy is inherently unstable: it is possible to believe that your chances of victory are higher if you strike first rather than if you wait. It is, however, important to stress that at the moment and in the near future the risks that either of the superpowers would be running by attacking first are very great indeed. To attempt to destroy the bulk of the other side's military forces in a surprise attack would be extremely hazardous. There are many uncertainties about whether missiles could actually be flown over the North Pole (the shortest route) and still hit their targets accurately. And there is great uncertainty about whether the other side would, as soon as it realised that it was being attacked, launch its own missiles without waiting for those of the attacker to arrive. Finally and most importantly, the submarines of the superpowers which carry

In 1980–81 there were several reported errors in the US computers which warn of a Soviet nuclear attack. It has been reported that such things as gas flares and flocks of birds have, at first, been mistaken for a Soviet missile attack. US defence spokesmen deny that their weapons could be fired accidentally or on the basis of incorrect computer data. But can we be so sure?

'WELL, DAMMIT, THAT'S NOT WHAT THIS PRINT-OUT SAYS!'

Strategic nuclear forces

These two graphs show that, although the number of platforms from which nuclear warheads can be launched (i.e. submarines, silos and aircraft) has stabilised, the actual numbers of warheads possessed by each side has increased dramatically. Note the drive by the Soviet Union after 1975 to catch up with the USA in warhead numbers.

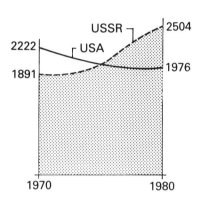

Numbers of launchers

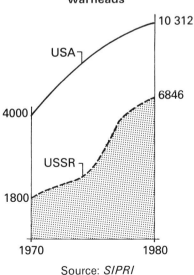

Numbers of warheads

Source: *SIPRI*

strategic missiles are still largely invulnerable to attack because they cannot be located when they are deep under the sea. But how long will the situation remain like this?

There are clear signs that both superpowers are actively working to develop technological improvements to overcome the problems outlined above. The USA is particularly advanced with new methods of detecting submarines, while the Russians have made great strides in developing killer satellites which can knock out enemy communication.

But undoubtedly, the biggest development in this area is the American Star Wars programme. Its supporters argue that current nuclear strategies cannot last for ever, and therefore the USA should begin to investigate the possibilities of new defence systems to replace the 'mutual suicide' of the present situation. The problem, however, is that Star Wars threatens to make arms control more difficult. An effective defensive shield possessed by both superpowers might enable them to negotiate away their offensive nuclear forces. But, along with Stars Wars developments, the USA is simultaneously increasing its offensive, war-fighting nuclear forces. In 1984, the US Secretary of Defense said:

> *If we can get a system which is effective and which we know can render their weapons impotent, we could be back in the situation when we were the only nation with a nuclear weapon.*

So it is hardly surprising that the Russians see Star Wars as part of a war-fighting strategy. This makes the Russians reluctant to agree to any limits on their strategic nuclear warheads. Rather, it encourages them to deploy ever larger numbers because that would be the best way of overwhelming any defensive screen that the USA might build and deploy.

The unremitting effort to develop new weapon systems is stimulated by mistrust of the other side. But it also helps to create further mistrust and fear since it can also be interpreted as preparation for attacking the other side's military capabilities. Counterforce strategy tends to accelerate the nuclear arms race. It encourages technological developments which endeavour to cancel out the efforts of each superpower. For example, as Soviet warheads have been made more accurate so the Americans have devised ways of making their missiles mobile and therefore less easy to target. But also, one way of answering the moves of the other side is simply to increase the number of weapons that have to be targeted, and both superpowers have been rapidly doing just that.

Counterforce strategy may be a better deterrent than MAD because it is more believable and a better threat, and therefore less likely ever to have to be used, but its main weakness is that it is unstable. There is no point where either side can call a halt and say, 'OK, we're strong enough; let's stop there'. Counterforce has a built-in momentum which encourages new and better methods of attack and defence to be devised, just as with conventional weapons, and encourages the production of more weapons to keep up with the other side. This serves to ensure that the nuclear arms race, like the conventional arms race, steadily gathers pace without increasing the security of either superpower; rather, the opposite is happening. And, it can be argued, counterforce makes nuclear war more likely because, risky though it may be to launch a first strike, it is even more risky not to be the first. And as the counterforce capabilities of both superpowers grow in the future, this instability will get worse.

7 The European theatre

The balance of forces

As we saw in the last chapter, the nuclear arms race has developed in several ways: increasing numbers of weapons, more accurate warheads, better control of weapons in war, and new methods of detecting enemy forces and missiles. Yet, however much effort is put into armaments, it often appears that people on each side believe that the other is ahead in some way. Arguments about defence are often conducted in public in the USA. In the Soviet Union, on the other hand, such things are done in secret, so we are only able to guess at what they are thinking. Reliable facts and figures are available about Western armed forces but, except for long-range nuclear weapons, information and statistics about Soviet weapons and forces are often little more than guesswork. As we saw in Chapter 5, it is often necessary for Western defence experts to guess what the Russians might be planning to do in the future on the basis of inadequate information about what they are doing at the moment.

In the late 1970s, concern grew in the West about the continuing build-up of Soviet military forces of all kinds. European leaders were anxious about new Soviet nuclear missiles targeted on Western Europe, and American experts were worried about all of the Soviet Union's new accurate missiles and its increased air lift and naval strengths. For their part, the Russians argued that NATO plans to modernise their nuclear forces and introduce new nuclear missiles into Europe, were merely continuing the arms race, whereas their own weapons build-up was designed to catch up with NATO. There is no doubt that each side has very real worries about the military strength of the other. It is possible to make out a good case for either side. It is not easy to say if either alliance is clearly ahead in the arms race. As the diagram on page 63 shows, NATO forces are superior in some ways, the Warsaw Pact in others.

Nevertheless, the Soviet Union is a mighty military power which has been growing stronger year by year. Fear of its growing strength was one reason for the NATO decisions taken in the late 1970s to increase defence spending each year and to modernise European theatre nuclear weapons which are regarded by many in NATO as the linchpin of the defence of Europe against any Soviet aggression. The French and British decided to modernise their own nuclear forces and at the same time *cruise* and *Pershing II* missiles were introduced into Europe, supposedly to counteract recent modernisation of Soviet missiles and missile defences. What was the background to these decisions?

Nuclear weapons come to Europe

At the end of the Second World War the middle of Europe marked the dividing line between East and West. Although it had been agreed during the war that the countries of Eastern Europe would be

NATO and Warsaw Pact forces compared

One of the reasons why NATO has relied a lot on nuclear weapons is their fear of Warsaw Pact superiority in conventional forces. The diagram shows part of the picture in 1986, excluding reinforcements. The survey* from which these figures were taken shows that the Warsaw Pact forces are greater in number in the air and on the ground, with a particular advantage in surface-to-surface missiles that could carry conventional, chemical or nuclear warheads deep into NATO territory. On the other hand NATO naval forces are generally superior (e.g. 13 aircraft carriers to 3).

However, it is wrong to make a simple comparison of numbers. There are other factors to be taken into account. NATO forces are loosely co-ordinated, and different countries use different equipment. This creates problems in working together. In contrast, Warsaw Pact forces use a common design and accept Soviet leadership. NATO forces are generally regarded as superior in technology and electronics. The effectiveness of the forces of the two alliances would also depend on the morale and organisation of the troops, upon the speed at which reinforcements could be brought in as well as upon where and when the fighting took place. Such things are not easy to measure.

Overall, the survey concludes, 'the conventional military balance...makes general military aggression a highly risky undertaking for either side... The consequences for an attacker would still be quite unpredictable, and the risks, particularly of nuclear escalation, quite incalculable.' Thus, if neither side can risk an attack, then there is a rough balance between them.

*Source: 'The Military Balance,' International Institute for Strategic Studies, 1986

NATO	Item	Warsaw Pact
2 779 000	total ground forces (manpower)	2 827 000
20 314	tanks	46 610
8974	artillery	3525
1811	anti-tank guided weapons	5365
786	surface-to-air missile launchers	5365
387	surface-to-surface missile launchers	1235
514	fighters and intercepters	2370
259	bombers	410
2435	ground attack aircraft	2216
714	armed helicopters	2085

Ranges of nuclear weapons

battlefield
tactical
theatre
strategic

Battlefield or *tactical* nuclear weapons are low yield, short-range weapons designed for use in a battle between opposing forces. The neutron bomb and the Lance missile are examples of these weapons.

Theatre nuclear weapons include all short-range and medium-range nuclear weapons for use within an area of military operations. Experts refer to Europe and the Middle East as possible theatres of nuclear war.

Strategic nuclear weapons are the long-range nuclear weapons, for instance those of the superpowers, which can hit each other's territory and war-making ability. Because many American nuclear weapons in the European theatre can strike deep into Soviet territory, the Russians regard them as part of the USA's strategic forces. In view of this, some people argue that there is no clear distinction between theatre and strategic weapons. These weapons are therefore sometimes referred to as *intermediate* or *Eurostrategic* weapons.

within the Soviet 'sphere of influence' after the end of the war, the military occupation of a whole belt of countries by Soviet forces and the installation by the Soviet Union of governments in these countries who would take their orders directly from Moscow, deeply alarmed Western leaders. The Russians wanted Eastern Europe as a buffer against any further invasion from the West and wanted to use the industries and resources of those countries that had helped Hitler, in order to rebuild the shattered Soviet economy. To achieve this, no risk of losing control could be taken, and the Russians imposed their will with an iron grip.

Would the massive forces of the Soviet Union be used to roll on into West Germany, France, Greece and the rest of Europe? In 1949 the Americans and several European nations formed the North Atlantic Treaty Organisation (NATO), clearly aimed to provide collective defence against any such Soviet aggression. In 1955 the Soviet Union and its Eastern European satellites responded by forming the Warsaw Pact, and shortly afterwards American nuclear weapons were stationed in Europe for the first time.

Nuclear weapons have, since their introduction in 1956, provided the basis of the NATO policy for defending Western Europe. They were adopted for two major reasons. First it was felt by the Western European nations that they could not hope to match the strength of Soviet conventional forces in Europe, and that it would be more effective and far cheaper for them to prevent any Soviet aggression by possessing a nuclear deterrent. Secondly it was felt to be necessary to strengthen this deterrent by underpinning the defence of Europe with an American guarantee to come to Western Europe's aid. This was to be achieved not only by basing American conventional forces in Western Europe, but also by having American nuclear weapons there. This would mean that the Soviet Union could not hope to attack Western Europe without risking a full-scale war with the USA.

The Russians developed their own nuclear weapons much more rapidly than anyone had originally expected. So, within a few years, Soviet nuclear weapons were being deployed in Eastern Europe too. Over the years, the numbers of nuclear weapons in Europe have steadily increased until, by the early 1980s, there were 6000 warheads in NATO hands and about 3000 in Warsaw Pact forces. In the mid 1980s, however, as part of the NATO modernisation programme, old warheads were replaced by new ones and the total stockpile was reduced to about 4600 warheads.

Flexible response

How might a war in Europe be fought if hostilities broke out between NATO and Warsaw Pact forces? It is commonly believed that the Warsaw Pact strategy would be to mount a massive attack upon NATO forces which would take the fighting onto NATO territory. The targets would, presumably, include the bases where nuclear weapons were stationed. Warsaw Pact forces would, it is expected, move forward to hold territory against the possibility of NATO reinforcement. Whether the Russians would use nuclear weapons at an early stage in such fighting, to knock out bases in Britain or to prevent the collecting of reinforcements, is not known, but it cannot be ruled out.

The NATO plan for resisting a Soviet invasion of Western Europe is known as '*flexible response*'. It involves a range of responses to

Flexible response

The official NATO strategy designed to deal with a Soviet invasion of Europe involves a 'ladder of escalation' or increasing force. it is doubtful whether, in such circumstances, the Soviet Union would equally gradually 'escalate' its use of force. The Russians have said that if the West uses nuclear weapons against them they will respond massively.

STAGE 4

This is the last card: global nuclear war. If all else fails, the Americans have guaranteed that they will be prepared to use their long-range strategic forces in support of Europe.

STAGE 3

At this stage, fairly large nuclear weapons, striking at the military and command centres of all the warring European nations and the Soviet Union, are involved. The hope is that, even at this stage, the war may be halted short of the total destruction of Europe. But if that does not happen the USA will come to Europe's aid with her strategic forces.

STAGE 2

NATO may use tactical nuclear weapons to knock out tank concentrations, key supply depots, marshalling yards etc. in the rear of the battlefield. Thus NATO forces will, if necessary, be the first to use nuclear weapons. If these measures fail to stop the war, or if the Warsaw Pact resorts to theatre nuclear weapons, STAGE 3 is reached.

STAGE 1

A Soviet conventional attack in Europe will be held back for as long as possible using NATO's conventional weapons. If this fails, or if the Warsaw Pact introduces nuclear weapons into the battle, then STAGE 2 is reached.

Soviet moves, from the use of conventional forces right up to the unleashing of US strategic nuclear missiles (see above).

Although there are strong doubts on the part of some European defence experts, in public it is argued that this policy of 'flexible response', employing as it does a graduated ladder of escalation, effectively deters any aggressive moves by Warsaw Pact forces because they know that NATO would match any level of force they could use. Many people believe that NATO's nuclear weapons provide the best way of defending Western Europe. They point to the fact that Soviet forces have not moved any further westwards since the end of the Second World War and argue that the West has its nuclear deterrent to thank for that. Many other people, however, remain unconvinced. They argue that the introduction of nuclear weapons into Europe by both sides has increased the chances that Europe might become a nuclear battlefield in a war between the superpowers.

These criticisms are founded on two main points. Many American nuclear weapons in Europe, whether based in West Germany or Britain or in ships and submarines, can reach the Soviet Union. It is not surprising therefore that the Russians tend to see these weapons as part of America's nuclear deterrent – the front line of its strategic defences. They cannot rule out the possibility that such weapons may be used against them in a conflict with the USA that breaks out in any part of the world. The Russians felt especially threatened by NATOs modernisation programme which, in the early 1980s, introduced 464 cruise missiles into various European countries and 108 Pershing II missiles into West Germany. The Pershing II carried the latest guidance systems and was designed to be accurate to a few metres. It was ideal for attacking hardened military targets and could be fitted with earth-penetrating warheads which could destroy underground command centres. From its launch in Germany a Pershing II missile would reach Moscow in about six minutes.

The Russians managed to secure the removal of both of these weapons systems in the Intermediate-range Nuclear Forces (INF) Treaty of 1987. This treaty was a landmark because it was the first ever agreement between the superpowers which meant a real *reduction* in warheads. The Americans agreed to withdraw land-based cruise and Pershing missiles, while the Russians agreed to withdraw their modern *SS*-20 and *SS*-23 missiles, and some older ones as well. In total the USA gave up 900 missiles, the USSR 3500. This represented about eight per cent of the world nuclear stockpile.

The treaty was a very significant step towards reducing the risk of war in Europe. It meant the removal of some of the most modern and threatening weapons, and it could mark the beginning of a slow process of disarmament. However, the treaty still leaves in place a large number of battlefield weapons in the front line. No doubt the longer range systems, including SBLMs, will have been retargeted to cover the targets of the removed systems. NATO governments, though supporting the treaty, still put their faith in nuclear deterrence and speak of the continued need to modernise. Such modernisation might involve fitting new weapons onto nuclear strike aircraft, and placing cruise missiles onto submarines. European NATO governments remain determined to prevent the Americans reducing their protective nuclear umbrella over Europe.

Protest against cruise missiles at Greenham Common, 1982

Ground-launched cruise missiles were introduced into Europe as part of NATO's modernisation programme. This provoked considerable public opposition. At one stage, thousands of protesters, mainly women, surrounded Greenham Common Airforce base in England where the first 96 cruise missiles were eventually deployed. The protesters failed to stop the deployment, but the presence of US nuclear forces on British soil continued to cause opposition from a large number of people in Britain.

Critics of NATOs weapons' policy still argue that any reliance on nuclear force in Europe is too risky. They say that limited nuclear war could easily escalate out of hand, and point out that only 200 of the thousands of nuclear weapons in Europe would be enough to destroy all its major cities. Europe could, they fear, experience a war in which the explosive force of up to 35 000 'Hiroshimas' was let loose. They are worried too that the superpowers might be able to settle their argument by using Europe as a battleground. Even were the superpowers to call a halt before they destroyed each other, that would be too late for the people of Europe.

Could Britain survive a nuclear war?

Britain plays a very important part in NATO defence strategy and would have many jobs to do in the event of a war in Europe. It has soldiers and airmen in Germany, sharing the front-line defence. Along with other navies, it has an important naval role in keeping open the sea routes across the Atlantic. Its air force has the job of defending the air space over a broad area of the eastern Atlantic. It provides bases and facilities for American forces – including nuclear bombers and submarines. Finally, it would be a major staging post for the reinforcement of US forces in Europe. Its airports and harbours would be very valuable to NATO in a conventional war because they would be far from the European front line.

If, however, a war in Europe should involve use of nuclear weapons, then Britain, because of the important role it plays in NATO, would be a very high priority target indeed. If deterrence were to break down and nuclear weapons were used in Europe (no matter who started it) Britain could expect a nuclear attack. Of course, nobody knows exactly what weapons the Russians would use against Britain in the event of war, nor where they would strike, nor whether they would attack all their targets simultaneously. Much would depend on whether NATO had struck first, whether this had been effective in knocking out many Soviet weapons, and on many other unknown factors. However, it is possible to get some idea of what an attack on Britain might involve. Earlier we looked at the consequences of just one nuclear bomb on one city. The map on page 68 shows 100 likely nuclear targets in the event of war, according to a civil defence exercise in 1980 which represented one view of what a nuclear attack on Britain would be like.

Could Britain survive a nuclear attack? The answer to this question is: it all depends. It depends on how big the attack is. It depends upon what kinds of civil defence measures are taken before the attack. It depends on who answers the question – because opinions differ widely on this topic. But finally it really depends on what is meant by the term 'survival'. It makes a lot of difference whether we take survival to mean the ability to more or less maintain and rebuild our way of life after an attack or whether by survival we mean some of us just being physically alive.

There can be no doubt that, if even a small fraction of the Soviet Union's nuclear warheads were used against Britain, it could be reduced to a smouldering radioactive ashpit.

What level of casualties could Britain expect? Estimates vary widely on this. The British government stated in 1980 that up to 30 million Britons might die in a nuclear war. This is about 56 per cent of the total population. However, it was also stated that if people were to follow simple government guidelines to protect themselves,

Probable nuclear targets in Britain

In the civil defence exercise called 'Operation Square Leg' from which this map was taken, it was assumed that over 100 targets were hit by warheads ranging in power from 0.5 megatons to 5 megatons. There was a mixture of airbursts and groundbursts, and of military and urban targets.

As the map shows, many large centres of population – such as Portsmouth, High Wycombe and Heathrow Airport – are near military targets which were attacked. This implies that in a counterforce attack upon Britain civilian casualties would be very high.

The map also shows the likely fallout pattern over the country 3 hours after the main attack on a day on which there was a gentle southerly breeze.

A detailed study (*London after the Bomb*, Greene et al, 1986) looked at the likely effects of the 5 warheads that fell around London in the 'Square Leg' attack. It concluded that 1 million people would die within seconds from the blast effects, and more than 4 million would die within the next 2 months from the effects of radiation.

(Map reproduced by permission from 'War Plan UK' by Duncan Campbell, Burnett Books 1982).

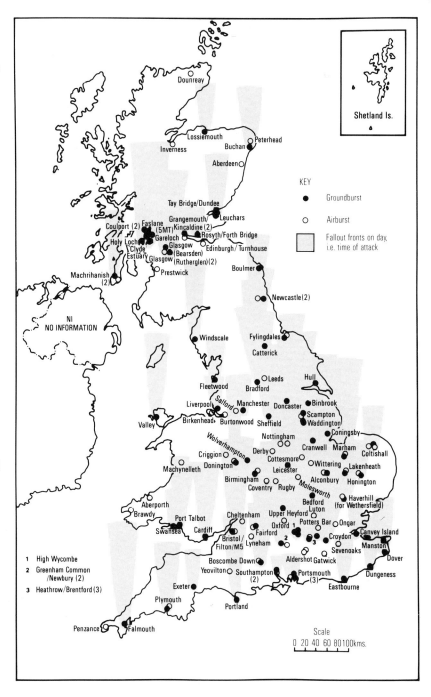

KEY

● Groundburst

○ Airburst

▢ Fallout fronts on day, i.e. time of attack

1 High Wycombe
2 Greenham Common /Newbury (2)
3 Heathrow/Brentford (3)

those people not affected by actual bomb blast would have a good chance of survival at least in the short term. As a result, deaths might be reduced from 30 to 15 million people, twenty-eight per cent of the population.

Other estimates are less optimistic. Some studies have suggested that casualties could be as high as 41 million killed or injured. In a study carried out for the Greater London Council (*London under attack*, R. Clarke, 1986) it was estimated that an attack on Britain involving 241 nuclear explosions would kill or injure fifty per cent of

What to do in the event of a nuclear attack: close all doors and windows, go to the downstairs middle room of the house, kneel, put both hands together...

the British population. More than eighty-five per cent of the population of London would be killed or injured and more than ninety per cent of London's housing stock made uninhabitable. The city would be reduced to rubble and would have to be abandoned. No set of civil defence measures could alter this outcome. In the end it is clearly very hard to say how many casualties there would be in a nuclear attack on Britain. One can say that many millions of people would be likely to perish and that the fabric of society would be completely destroyed. But could a better civil defence policy protect the population against the effects of nuclear war?

Civil defence

Since 1962 every new house built in Switzerland has had to have a nuclear blast and fallout shelter fitted into a deep basement. The shelter must be constructed of thick concrete and steel. It must be fitted with a blast door and an air filtering system. It also has to be stocked with food, medical supplies and clothing. It must be big enough for the whole family and have a little room to spare for a guest! For those houses built before 1962, for children at school, for people at work or on journeys, there are communal shelters in public places throughout the country. Every village has a communal shelter complete with food, beds, diesel generators, air filters and first aid equipment. There are hundreds of underground hospitals complete with operating theatres ready to be brought into action at a few hours' notice. There are also underground fire stations and ambulance depots. Every Swiss citizen is taught and practices what to do in the event of a nuclear war. Switzerland is a neutral country. It has no nuclear weapons. It has kept itself clear of the rival military alliances in Europe. Its armed forces are designed for defence of territory only and are not a threat to Switzerland's neighbours. Yet the Swiss people have taken very seriously indeed the threat of nuclear war being brought down on their heads by the actions of their warring neighbours.

Swiss shelters are also built to withstand the blast wave of a one-megaton groundburst 2.5 kilometres away. The Swiss do not themselves expect to be direct targets in a nuclear war, but nuclear weapons could be used against forces that had occupied Swiss territory, or they may be used to prevent valuable resources falling into enemy hands. So, to guard against this eventuality, the Swiss have ensured that, by the end of this century, everybody and everything of value in the country will be protected from anything short of a direct hit by a nuclear warhead. In 1982 the Swiss spent $339 per person on defence. $28 of this went on civil defence. In the same year Britain spent $488 per person, of which about $2 went on civil defence.

No other country in the world, except for Sweden, has as developed a civil defence system as Switzerland. Certainly, no other country possesses an underground shelter system that could protect most of the population in a nuclear war. Such a system for Britain could cost as much as $117 billion, which is nearly five times its total annual defence budget. Civil defence programmes in all NATO countries have been minimal, and would provide very little protection for their populations, despite recent increases in civil defence spending. Both China and the Soviet Union take civil defence more seriously. The Soviet Union has, according to most experts on the subject, certainly built underground shelters for key workers and

Swiss blast and fallout shelter

Swiss shelters are built to very high standards. By the end of the century every person in Switzerland will have access to one wherever he or she may be in time of crisis.

administrators and for military and political leaders. There are plans to evacuate people from likely target areas if war threatened. As usual in assessments of the Soviet Union, there is widespread disagreement about the extent and effectiveness of its civil defence measures. However, some recent studies argue that the Russians lack the transport for a mass evacuation and have never rehearsed one. They doubt if there are enough materials available for people to build makeshift shelters in the countryside once they had been evacuated. They also point out that most key industries in the Soviet Union are concentrated in particular areas so that most of the Soviet economy could not escape destruction in a nuclear war.

It is doubtful whether any of the countries with nuclear weapons could protect their industries or many of their people from the effects of nuclear explosions. (For the government of a country which possesses nuclear weapons to embark upon a major civil defence programme is to admit that its policy of nuclear deterrence may not work.) If such a country began to move large numbers of people out of its cities in an international crisis this could easily be spotted by satellites. It would definitely be interpreted to mean that the country was preparing to go to war and such actions could therefore invite an attack to knock out their forces before they were ready to use them. Is it for this reason that, during the Cuban missile crisis in 1962 none of the nuclear-weapons states involved activated any civil defence measures? Such moves might have made war more likely.

Consequences of an attack on Britain

In the 1950s the British Government decided that it would be impossible to protect the mass of the British people from the effects of a nuclear attack. That was still the government's position in the early 1980s. They advised ordinary householders to stay at home and to build, if they could, makeshift refuges inside their homes to protect them from fallout. It is clear from what we have said about nuclear explosions in Chapter 3, and about the kind of attack that could be expected as described in this chapter, that over vast areas of the country such measures would give very little protection indeed.

Up to 4.5 kilometres from each of the 125 explosions expected, people's homes and inner refuges would simply collapse around them. Out to a distance of 12 kilometres (an area of 450 sq km around every explosion) houses would be sufficiently badly damaged for the deadly radioactive fallout dust to blow through broken windows and through cracks in the roof and walls, to land on the refuge and to be inhaled, or to trickle onto people's heads when it rained. In such conditions people could, within a day, receive enough radiation to kill them. Between 12 kilometres and 40 kilometres from each explosion more people would be likely to survive in their home-made refuges especially if their roofs were still intact and if they had managed to brick their windows up. But they would still be likely to suffer from radiation sickness – vomiting, diarrhoea and bleeding. They would have to remain in their refuge for at least two weeks. They would need enough food and water for

Government advice on 'do-it-yourself' protection from nuclear attack

The government's booklet *Protest and Survive*, first published in 1980, has been strongly criticised by those who say that it underestimates the destructive power of nuclear explosions, and greatly overestimates the protection against fallout that people's homes would give them. The booklet was also criticised for ignoring the threat to life caused by the destruction of agriculture, health care and other public services in the weeks and months after a nuclear attack.

According to one study, based on the 'Square Leg' exercise, 85 per cent of London's 'home-made' shelters, as recommended by the government, would be destroyed by blast, leaving the population unprotected from fire and radiation effects.

In 1986 the Home Secretary said that a revised version of the booklet had been prepared but the government had decided not to publish it in case people refused to take it seriously. Partly as a result of public criticism of civil defence, the government began to place a greater emphasis upon emergency planning to provide defence against a wide range of disasters such as major accidents or chemical leaks rather than nuclear wars alone.

this time and somewhere to put their waste. There would be no electricity, no gas, no heating, no running water, no medical help and probably no information since nuclear explosions damage most radio equipment for hundreds of kilometres around. Nor would they know, as they sat cramped in their refuge little bigger than a cupboard, whether the war had ended, whether help would come, or even whether they would live since they would not be able to tell how much radiation they were receiving. They might have to watch helplessly as someone, perhaps a child, died in terrible agony, over a period of days or weeks. This is a truly horrible picture; but it would happen to the people of any country attacked with nuclear weapons if the population lacked purpose-built protection of a very high standard.

Nothing can survive a direct hit by a nuclear warhead. But the best protection is afforded by underground solid structures reinforced with steel or concrete. Such shelters can be bought, but they are expensive and few people can afford them. In 1980 the British government publicly stated that it would be too expensive to provide everyone with a proper blast and fallout shelter. However, in order to ensure that the government is still able to operate, make decisions and fight the war in the event of nuclear attack, there are a number of specially-built deep shelters throughout Britain to which political leaders and about 20 000 key administrators would be sent if war seemed imminent. Should war occur, these people would take over the government of vast regions of the country and would try to provide help, order and organisation for the survivors afterwards. Top government officials and the military also have their own bunkers, for directing the country's military forces during a nuclear war. So, according to present plans, on the eve of a nuclear war, the government, top civil servants and military leaders would disappear underground, leaving the rest of the population to fend for themselves.

Heartless as this may seem, it is partly a reflection of the massive costs that would be involved in the construction of underground

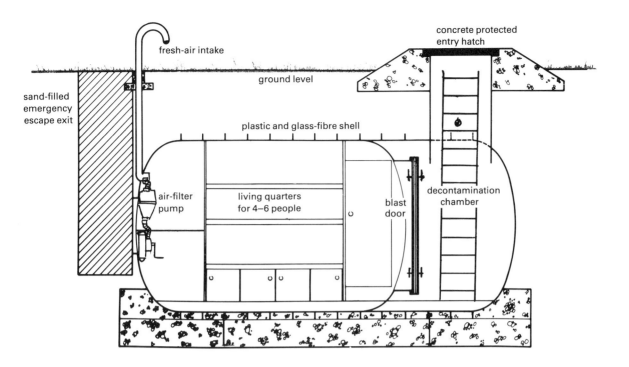

Labels in figure:
- fresh-air intake
- concrete protected entry hatch
- ground level
- sand-filled emergency escape exit
- plastic and glass-fibre shell
- air-filter pump
- living quarters for 4–6 people
- blast door
- decontamination chamber

An example of a high-quality British domestic nuclear shelter

This kind of nuclear blast and fallout shelter could be lowered onto concrete foundations and covered with earth. It would protect people from blast effects if they were more than 2–3 km from the centre of the explosion. They might, however, be asphyxiated if widespread fires consumed the available oxygen.

Such a shelter could provide complete protection from fallout and chemical weapons for as long as the occupants stayed underground. How long they could stay underground would depend on food supply and whether anyone else was trying to get in! Very few people in Britain have anything like this protection; and they will have had to pay between £20 000 and £50 000 for the privilege.

shelters that might be of limited value in a country with so many direct targets. The government shelters are part of the deterrent strategy. As we saw earlier a deterrent is only useful if the enemy can be persuaded that their opponents could and would use it. The protection of the government and military ensures that they would survive to conduct such a war and be able to give orders to their nuclear forces such as the *Polaris* or *Trident* submarines. This, it is argued, makes Britain's nuclear deterrent more credible, stronger and therefore more likely to ensure peace.

It seems clear that, for a country with nuclear weapons on its territory, civil defence can offer very little protection for the general population. According to one writer:

> *Survival will not be home and family, nor neighbours, lovers, colleagues and friends. Survival is not health, hope or happiness. Survival will be fear, exhaustion, disease, pain and long, lonely misery.* (James Lewis in *London Under Attack* by R. Clarke)

Many people argue that civil defence only makes sense in a country that does not expect to be a major target in a nuclear war; otherwise it is simply an effort to provide people with a false sense of security so that they will not object to preparations for war-fighting.

Global consequences

Even a limited nuclear exchange could have devastating effects over wide areas of the globe. Clouds of radioactive fallout would drift and fall onto countries not involved in the fighting. Trade, agriculture and industry would be disrupted or destroyed. The USA, for example, produces most of the grain that feeds the hungry in the Third World; and some of it even goes to feed the Russians! The economic collapse of countries could result in large numbers of

The nuclear winter

Nuclear explosions cause huge fires in cities, oil storage depots and forests. Large amounts of smoke and dust blot out the light from the sun, resulting in falling temperatures.

Temperatures fall rapidly: summer turns to winter.

After a few weeks the huge dust cloud begins to drift into the southern hemisphere, leading to the destruction of the delicate balance of nature across much of the planet.

deaths from starvation and disease in many parts of the world not directly involved in the fighting.

Some scientists have predicted that nuclear explosions, even on a small scale could dramatically change the world's weather patterns. Nuclear explosions cause widespread fires and hurl massive quantities of dust and debris into the upper atmosphere. This produces a dense blanket of dust and smoke that gradually spreads across the sky. The sun's heat cannot get through it. The surface of the earth cools rapidly. Summer could turn to winter – across huge areas of the earth's surface – in what is termed the *nuclear winter*.

8 Halting the arms race

Arms control and disarmament

In the first chapter of this book we quoted a section of the Final Document of the United Nations *Special Session on Disarmament* in 1978. It clearly states how important it is to halt the arms race and to achieve disarmament. It was signed by 149 of the world's governments including the superpowers and all other nuclear-weapons countries. Many of the world's leaders have publicly declared that the arms race is madness and have committed themselves to seeking disarmament. The Soviet Union and the USA are solemnly bound by international treaties to seek complete nuclear disarmament and they have even made proposals for general disarmament which have not subsequently been withdrawn. And yet despite this awareness of the problems caused by the arms race, and despite their public commitment to disarmament, governments have continued to increase their armaments faster than before. As we have seen, the superpowers doubled the number of their nuclear warheads in the 1970s, a decade that was named by the United Nations as 'the disarmament decade'. Moreover, the superpowers increased the number of their nuclear warheads even further between 1980 and 1986. Why is there such a contrast between the stated intentions of governments and their actual behaviour?

There have been many attempts in the past to control armaments. Most of them have failed. In trying to explain why it has proved so difficult to achieve disarmament, we must consider several obstacles which appear to have blocked progress time and time again:

Doing it alone or with others?

A *unilateral* decision is one that is taken by one side only. For example, decisions by a country to increase its armaments are taken unilaterally. When referring to disarmament, the term unilateral means that one country or side decides to reduce arms levels no matter what other countries decide to do.

This is usually contrasted with *multilateral* disarmament. In that situation, disarmament measures are taken by several countries who agree together the steps they will take. However, many people argue that unilateral reductions are a necessary first step towards multilateral disarmament.

Obstacles to disarmament

1 It is easier to make unilateral moves than to reach an agreement with others. Therefore it is easier to make a decision to increase armaments than to try to agree with others to decrease them.

2 The more countries there are involved in the discussions, the more difficult it is to reach an agreement.

3 Disarmament is unfamiliar. Reliance on armed force goes back for centuries. It is easier to rely on the familiar than to venture into the unknown.

4 If the arms to be reduced are similar on both sides, then agreement may be relatively straightforward. But if different types of arms are to be reduced on each side this creates problems. It is often difficult to decide upon which arms to include in an agreement and which to leave out.

5 Disarmament must not leave either side feeling at a military disadvantage to the other, at any stage. Equal staged reductions by all involved may be the best way of achieving this. But if they are not equal to start with or cannot agree on the relative size and strength of their armaments, it makes agreement very difficult.

Approaches to halting the arms race

Putting the brakes on

Arms control and *arms limitations* both refer to a policy of restricting the deployment of existing weapons or the development of new ones. Neither necessarily involves a reduction in the total number or range of armaments already held. SALT was an example of arms control.

Putting the arms race into reverse

Disarmament means a reduction in the total number of arms held by a country or group of countries. It may be forcibly carried out as when a defeated enemy is forcibly disarmed by the victors or it may be voluntary.

Taking others along

When arms control or disarmament talks are being conducted between a group of countries, they are known as *multilateral* negotiations. When only two countries are involved, as in the SALT talks between the USA and the Soviet Union, the talks are called *bilateral*.

Checking up on cheating

One of the major difficulties in reaching agreement on arms control or disarmament is how to check that the terms of the agreement are being fulfilled by all parties to it. This is known as verification. There is no 100 per cent certain means of *verification*. On-site inspection of military facilities or weapons before and after dismantling is one way of checking. But satellites with high-resolution cameras can do quite a good job. However, as nuclear weapons are becoming more numerous and much smaller in size, verification will become increasingly difficult.

6 It must be possible to check or verify that the other side is not cheating. This is often very difficult and can ruin the chances of agreement, especially if there is little trust between the various parties. There is, of course, no way of actually forcing the other side to keep to its promises.

7 The military establishments of countries are very reluctant to give up anything. They usually put pressure on their governments not to make concessions. If there is little public interest in the negotiations, the military groups can have an overwhelming influence.

8 It is much more difficult to disarm (i.e. to get rid of weapons) than to agree to limited arms control (i.e. to restrict the use of present weapons or the development of new ones). Indeed, arms control agreements may act as a 'cloak' to hide a failure to achieve real disarmament.

9 Countries are unwilling to forego the development and deployment of new weapons systems if they believe that those systems might give them an advantage or help them overcome a weakness. Such developments can also undermine existing arms treaties.

Arms control efforts since 1945

Since 1945 the United Nations has been the major organisation trying to achieve disarmament. In 1952 the Soviet Union proposed to the UN that the world's major powers should cut their armed forces by one third each. The Western nations rejected this because it would have involved them in making the bigger actual cuts. They suggested instead reductions in smaller steps down to agreed maximum numbers for each country. Proposals and counterproposals went to and fro between the Western nations and the Russians. The Russians in particular wanted the Americans to get rid of all their nuclear weapons before they would reduce their own conventional forces. The West wanted things the other way. (This is an example of **obstacle 4**). The Russians had, for many years, refused to allow inspection of their military facilities by outsiders in case they be used to spy and get other information. But by 1955 an outline agreement for reductions in conventional forces and eventual abolition of nuclear weapons had been formulated and the Russians had even agreed to allow inspection of their military facilities. But, for reasons which even today remain unclear, the Americans suddenly drew out and said that they did not believe it would be possible to verify that the Russians were keeping to the agreement (**obstacle 6**). They suggested unrestricted satellite photography of each other's territory and small-scale limited agreements. But the Russians were not interested in those proposals. The talks collapsed and no further efforts were made to achieve such a widespread disarmament. Indeed, as we saw in earlier chapters, the opposite happened. Political leaders in both superpowers adopted new, more aggressive policies concerning armaments and the power and influence of the military–industrial complex increased. By the late 1950s the superpowers were ready to embark upon a massive escalation of the arms race (**obstacle 7**).

The superpowers did not, however, stop talking to each other, and in the 1960s a number of limited but important agreements were signed. These were, on the whole, agreements to restrict armaments. Only the *Biological Weapons Convention* of 1972 involved actual disarmament measures. The superpowers were not prepared to consider actual reduction in their own weapons (**obstacle 8**). And under pressure from their own military establishments even those treaties that were agreed were often weakened (**obstacles 5, 7** and **9**). For example, in the process of developing new nuclear weapons, the major powers had, for many years, carried out nuclear test explosions in the atmosphere. These produced immense amounts of radioactive fallout which spread around the globe. As more was learned of the dangers of radioactivity, alarm and opposition grew throughout the world. There were many calls for a complete ban on all nuclear weapons testing. But the superpowers were unwilling to agree to a comprehensive ban. Their weapons designers and military leaders told their political masters that if testing were stopped, it would be impossible to improve their nuclear weapons and their deterrent could not be developed further.

As a compromise, therefore, a *Partial Test Ban Treaty* was signed in 1963. This banned testing in the atmosphere, but it allowed testing to continue underground. This was acceptable to the military establishments within the superpowers (and in Britain) because they could continue to develop and test new weapons. As the diagram on page 78 shows, testing has not been reduced. The French and Chinese have refused to limit their freedom to explode nuclear weapons in the atmosphere claiming that to do so would inhibit the development of their nuclear weapons. So here we can see **obstacles 3, 5, 7** and **9** in operation.

In 1980 the Americans walked out of talks they had been involved in with the Russians and British about banning tests altogether. In August 1985 the Russians unilaterally suspended nuclear weapons testing and publicly called for a complete ban on nuclear tests by all countries. The USA and other countries refused to join, claiming that it would be impossible to check on whether the Russians were cheating. But technological improvements now make it possible to detect even the smallest explosions. The US government argued that it would be necessary to continue testing nuclear weapons as long as such weapons exist. The Soviet Union resumed testing in 1987.

Within the United Nations there has always been very strong support for disarmament from the vast majority of member countries. Every year a number of proposals are put forward for arms control and disarmament, but few ever get anywhere. The Soviet Union has put forward several very sweeping proposals. These have usually been dismissed by the West as 'propaganda' with little substance in them, though whether this is true is very hard for outsiders to judge.

The United Nations gradually lost its position at the centre of disarmament negotiations as the superpowers entered their own bilateral talks from the late 1960s onwards. These became known as the *Strategic Arms Limitation Talks* (or SALT).

The SALT talks made some progress. In 1972 the Russians and Americans agreed to limit the number of ABM systems to two on each side and an upper ceiling was placed on missile launchers. The next round of talks (SALT II) proved more difficult. In this round, limits were to be placed on certain kinds of weapons (ICBMs, SLBMs, bombers, MIRVed warheads and so on) so that each superpower could reach a ceiling where they would be equal with one another. But there were many problems characteristic of all arms control talks. There were difficulties in agreeing which weapons to include (**obstacle 4**). It was difficult to compare Soviet and US weapons

Nuclear test explosions 1945–85

Between July 1945 and the end of 1985, 1570 nuclear test explosions were carried out. Eighty-seven per cent of these tests were carried out by the superpowers as they worked to improve their nuclear warheads. The Partial Test Ban Treaty, signed in 1963, did nothing to reduce the *number* of tests. Twice as many tests were carried out in the 23 years since 1963 as in the 17 years before. But the treaty did reduce the amount of global nuclear fallout in the atmosphere. Even here, however, success has not been total. 22 of China's 29 tests and 41 of France's 126 tests since 1963 have been carried out in the atmosphere.

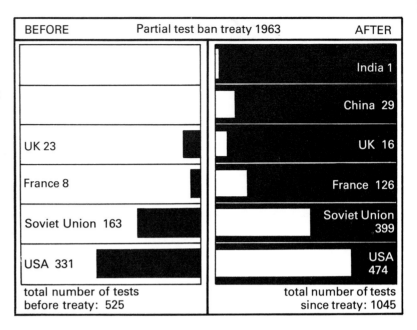

BEFORE	Partial test ban treaty 1963	AFTER
		India 1
		China 29
UK 23		UK 16
France 8		France 126
Soviet Union 163		Soviet Union 399
USA 331		USA 474
total number of tests before treaty: 525		total number of tests since treaty: 1045

because their type and proportions were so different (see diagram on page 59). The Russians were not prepared to forgo any developments the Americans had already made (**obstacle 9**) and so had to be allowed to increase the number of MIRVed warheads until they reached the number the USA had. The military–industrial complex in each country showed its usual unwillingness to give up what weapons it already had (**obstacle 7**), and so the SALT upper limits had to be set high enough to allow both sides to introduce new weapons already in the pipeline. The SALT agreements signed in 1979 allowed both superpowers to increase their nuclear armaments by up to fifty per cent. And all the while, new, more advanced weapons were being tested in the weapons laboratories. The Russians had a new bomber and a new submarine, the Americans had the cruise missile and a new ICBM. The military leaders on both sides argued that they just had to have those new systems if their country's security were to survive the restrictions of SALT. And so SALT was not allowed to put a stop to the technological improvements of weapons systems in the 1970s which introduced new, more accurate weapons (**obstacles 1** and **7**).

Nevertheless, there was mounting criticism within the USA of the SALT limits which, it was argued, allowed Russia to get ahead. When the Russians invaded Afghanistan in December 1979, President Carter shelved the SALT II agreement which had been signed only a few months earlier, but had not been approved by Congress. In 1980 when Ronald Reagan became the next President he dropped the SALT process altogether and introduced a massive arms build-up of both conventional and nuclear weapons. The new US government argued that the previous administrations had allowed America's defence to become weak and that the Soviet Union was so superior in all kinds of arms that about $1.5 trillion had to be spent over the next five years if the USA were to catch up. So much for twelve years of arms talks!

MOVES TOWARDS DISARMAMENT

Some of the ideas that have been put forward for a more peaceful world

FREEZE
An agreement to freeze all nuclear weapons numbers at present levels. No more weapons testing. No technological innovations. No more production of plutonium or uranium for weapons.

NUCLEAR-FREE ZONES
The creation of areas of the world completely free from nuclear weapons. This would eliminate tactical and theatre weapons. The nuclear weapons of the superpowers would be withdrawn into their own territories thereby restoring the role of nuclear weapons as strategic deterrents.

MULTILATERAL AGREEMENTS
Agreement to reduce or eliminate particular kinds of nuclear weapons: e.g. those useful for surprise attack and battlefield nuclear weapons. Another approach is to halt developments which weaken the other side's deterrent: e.g. anti-submarine surveillance.

UNILATERAL INITIATIVES
Smaller nuclear weapons states unilaterally reduce or abandon their nuclear weapons as a lead to others. Either superpower could show goodwill by making unilateral reductions to its arsenal without demanding equivalent cuts from the other.

PROLIFERATION BAN
A total ban on the export to any other country of nuclear weapons or the means of making them. Strict controls on the production, use and transportation of all nuclear fuels.

CHEMICAL DISARMAMENT
A complete ban on the development, testing, production, storage and use of any chemical weapons. All existing stocks to be destroyed.

SPACE DISARMAMENT
A total ban on the placing of any weapons in orbit or on planets, space stations, satellites, etc. This would halt laser, particle-beam and anti-satellite developments, but *not* intelligence and communications satellites.

ARMS TRADE RESTRICTIONS
International agreement to restrict the trade in arms: banning high-technology transfers, banning sales to areas of great tension; no sales to countries where that would alter the 'balance' in a particular region. Domestic arms industries converted to other production.

CONVENTIONAL FORCE REDUCTIONS
Agreed reductions of armed forces (men and equipment) to fixed levels for each country and in particular geographical areas. Strict limits to naval and air strengths and areas where these forces may operate.

MINIMUM DETERRENCE
The nuclear arsenals of both superpowers are reduced to the minimum levels required for mutual assured destruction. These weapons to be carried in invulnerable nuclear submarines. Both superpowers stop developments which make it easier to locate the other's submarines.

WORLD GOVERNMENT
A greatly strengthened United Nations to co-ordinate and organise comprehensive disarmament and ensure international compliance with the agreements reached. The UN also to act to help resolve world problems which lead to conflict.

ALTERNATIVE DEFENCE
Existing small nuclear-weapons states to abandon them completely and rely instead on modern conventional forces and/or guerrilla territorial defence.

The summit meeting in Iceland in 1986, between Reagan and Gorbachev, leaders of the two most powerful states on earth, led to the signing of the first ever nuclear disarmament treaty in Washington a year later.

During the early 1980s relations between the superpowers were very icy and no progress was made in arms control. The arms build-up in both superpowers and the modernisation of nuclear forces in Europe added to the gloom. In the mid 1980s, tensions eased and the leaders of the two superpowers met at summit talks.

These talks led to the signing of a treaty at the end of 1987. It abolished all land-based nuclear missiles in Europe in the range of 500 to 5500 km possessed by either superpower. The treaty was a very important one. Because it involved an agreement to *reduce* weapon stocks – rather than simply to limit future increases – it brought the superpowers into constructive dialogue and opened up the possibility of going much further in the future.

The signing of the treaty increased hopes of a future agreement on long-range strategic weapons, involving a possible cut of up to fifty per cent of stockpiles on both sides. Such a cut would be a massive move in the reversal of the arms race. Viewed in this way, the INF Treaty was more important for what it made possible than for what it actually achieved.

Nevertheless, there were many voices within the USA (and, no doubt, within the USSR) that were raised against any kind of deal with the other side. A very serious obstacle to further progress on disarmament continued to be American commitment to its Star Wars programme (**obstacle 9**), and Western European concerns about the size of Soviet conventional forces.

How was it possible to conclude a disarmament treaty in 1987, having failed so many times before? Some people argued that the Russians were forced to negotiate because of the NATO modernisation and build-up of weapons. Others put it down to President Reagan's desire to be viewed as a peace-maker. Another view was that President Gorbachev wanted to shift resources away from military spending and towards developing other elements of the Soviet economy. Probably all of these factors played a part, as did the role of the peace movement in the early 1980s.

The peace movement

The failure of the SALT talks, the rise in international tension following the Soviet invasion of Afghanistan and the fall of the Shah in Iran, together with NATO's plans to modernise its theatre nuclear weapons, and Britain's own plans to replace Polaris with a new submarine fleet all occurred within the space of eighteen months at the beginning of the 1980s. In that time there grew up in many West European countries massive popular movements against the arms race, particularly where nuclear weapons were involved. For many

The early 1980s saw a rapid growth in the peace movement in Europe and America. Millions of ordinary people marched on the streets and participated in campaigns to alert people to the dangers of nuclear war and to oppose the nuclear policies of their governments.

years there had been people campaigning against such things, but it was as if people across Europe were suddenly awakened to what had been going on for the past ten years or so. For years they had been told that the two superpowers had agreed to live at peace with one another and to curb their armaments. Instead they had increased their arsenals and were now snarling at each other. Growing numbers of people in Europe began to feel that their governments had allowed themselves to become pawns in the power game between the superpowers, and that nuclear weapons in Europe, far from protecting them actually increased their peril.

These and many other reasons lay behind the dramatic upsurge of opposition to nuclear weapons and the arms race in general that emerged throughout Europe in the early 1980s. There were huge marches in several European capitals. These marches expressed the fears of many millions and their lack of faith in the nuclear deterrent to keep the peace. Many organisations grew up both in Europe and the USA to put pressure upon governments to draw back from the arms race. Many politicians, diplomats, trade unionists and even some former top military men, joined the call to oppose the arms race.

The growth of these mass movements of opposition to the defence planning of the West shook those governments whose plans and decisions had always been taken in secret and which had hitherto aroused little opposition from a population which was apathetic or took the view that 'the experts know best'. Now, all such decisions were questioned; opposition political parties began to be far more critical of nuclear defence policies. Pressure began to increase upon governments to make some progress in achieving disarmament, particularly where nuclear weapons were concerned. In many European countries, such as Britain, West Germany and the Netherlands, considerable public and political opposition to nuclear weapons has developed, though in general, the mass protests have declined in recent years.

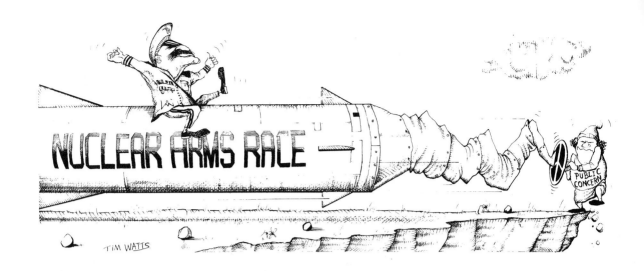

TiM WATTS

Britain and the bomb

After the Americans and the Russians, Britain was the first country to develop its own nuclear weapons. At first Britain's nuclear weapons were carried in bomber aircraft but, by the end of the 1960s, Britain's strategic deterrent was based on Polaris missile-carrying submarines. Although Britain now has a wide range of nuclear weapons as part of its contribution to NATO, Polaris is known as Britain's 'independent strategic deterrent'.

As the result of an agreement signed in 1962, the Americans have provided the missiles and other equipment for the four Polaris submarines while the British have built the submarines and the warheads. Although the Polaris force is assigned to NATO as part of a wider European defensive strategy, the British government reserves the right to use its Polaris missiles in a 'supreme national crisis'. This presumably means that, if there were a Soviet missile attack on Britain, it could retaliate independently of the rest of NATO including the Americans.

In 1980 the Government argued that if Britain's nuclear deterrent was to be able to penetrate Russian defences beyond the 1990s, it would have to be 'modernised'. It was decided to replace Polaris with the much more modern and powerful Trident system recently developed in the United States. At the same time, *Tornados* began to replace the aging V-bomber force. Opponents of British nuclear modernisation argued that Britain cannot afford and does not need to expand its nuclear capabilities by the massive amount that the Trident programme would yield. Some argued for a more limited modernisation, based perhaps on cruise missiles or on the Tornado multi-role combat aircraft. Yet others argued that Britain should take Polaris out of service and get rid of US nuclear bases altogether.

Opposition to Britain's possession of nuclear weapons grew rapidly in the early 1980s and the membership of anti-nuclear peace organisations such as the Campaign for Nuclear Disarmament increased enormously. Many prominent people including considerable numbers of MPs supported the aims of CND. In both the 1983 and 1987 elections the British Labour Party compaigned on a programme that committed them to a non-nuclear defence policy if they were elected.

The Trident missile-carrying submarine was the planned replacement for the aging Polaris system that the British government chose in the early 1980s.

A simple comparison between Polaris and Trident.

	Polaris	*Trident D5*
warheads per missile	3	14
range	4,000 km	12,000 km
accuracy against target	914 m	228 m
missiles per submarine	16	24
warheads per submarine	48	336

The main argument put forward by the peace campaigners was that, by having nuclear weapons, Britain was running an increasing risk of being destroyed in a nuclear war. They argued that, rather than waiting until all sides could agree on terms for multilateral disarmament. Britain should lead the way in stopping the arms race by getting rid of its weapons first – 'unilateral nuclear disarmament'.

The peace movement was not united in all its policies. Most campaigners wanted to go further than British nuclear disarmament and get rid of all US nuclear bases in Britain. Some wanted Britain to leave NATO altogether and become a neutral state like Sweden. For some people, nuclear disarmament would have to be balanced by an increased reliance on conventional weapons, while for others, it was just the first step towards general and complete disarmament. Also although some believed that Britain could and should act on its own, others wanted to link Britain with a wider movement which aimed to eliminate nuclear weapons from Europe as a whole.

Despite these differences, all were against Britain's nuclear weapons. On page 86 we see some of the most common arguments put forward by the peace campaigners. On page 87 are some of the views of those who favour the keeping of Britain's nuclear deterrent.

What are the chances for peace?

In the first chapter of this book it was suggested that there are no easy answers to this question. There are, as we have seen, many causes of the arms race and many forces propelling it onward. There are also many obstacles in the path of disarmament. There can be little doubt about the size of the task facing those who want to reverse the arms race, or about the length and difficult nature of the disarmament process with all its risks, disappointments and setbacks. But the ultimate goal is surely worthwhile: a world in which the risks of massive destruction from nuclear weapons have been reduced to nil, and a world in which the resources that currently go into the arms race can be freed for economic and social development. Such a freeing of resources to tackle the desperate problems of world poverty, disease, illiteracy and the shortages of energy and resources would go a long way towards reducing those conflicts which at present do so much to fuel the arms race. What steps may reasonably be taken to slow down and then reverse the arms race?

Ideas for reversing the arms race must begin with nuclear weapons, regarded by many as the greatest single threat to world peace. Here the core of the problem is the poor relationship between the USA and the Soviet Union. Unless their mutual hostility and fear can be reduced and replaced by efforts to improve co-operation and understanding between them, there can be little hope of progress.

But urgent measures must also be taken to deal directly with the arms competition between the superpowers, particularly where nuclear weapons are concerned. As we have seen, the nuclear arms race has developed its own internal logic which is leading towards ever more sophisticated war-fighting weapons systems and increasing warhead numbers. Such developments do nothing to increase the long-term security of either superpower, but do a great deal to increase the anxiety of each about what the other may be planning. So here, perhaps, is the point at which the central arms race between the superpowers can be halted.

Many different schemes have been put forward. Some involve withdrawing or reducing the most 'dangerous' weapons in the front lines in Europe, such as those like the Pershing missiles. Others call for an agreement on both sides to halt completely the development and testing of new weapon systems. To this could be added an interim agreement to freeze all nuclear weapons numbers as a prelude to talks about step-by-step reductions on both sides. Such moves could be strengthened by commitments from both superpowers not to be the first to use nuclear weapons. This all sounds easy, but it is far from straightforward.

We have seen how new technological developments are constantly in the pipeline, and are felt to be needed to catch up with or keep ahead of the other side. Any move to put a stop to all such developments would be strongly resisted by the military–industrial complex. Any move to freeze nuclear weapons numbers at the present level would invite criticism from one side about being left weaker than the other side. The SALT talks between the superpowers got bogged down over these kinds of issues. If such problems are to be overcome both superpowers need the political will to do so: the strong desire for talks to succeed and a belief that success will yield better results than failure. The failure of the SALT talks seems to imply that there was not enough support for disarmament. There were very strong forces at work in the USA, at least, arguing against 'giving away too much'. This view is strengthened by the recent history of disarmament proposals put forward by both the Russians and Americans which seem at first sight to offer real opportunities for arms reduction. But usually closer inspection has revealed that they involve much greater sacrifices and risks for one side than the other. It might be that such proposals are put forward simply for propaganda purposes. Nevertheless some serious and quite workable proposals emerged in the late 1980s.

If these barriers are to be overcome it seems that massive popular pressure will be required to make politicians take disarmament talks seriously. If such pressure can be applied and political leaders emerge who genuinely want to succeed, then progress will be much more likely than it has been in the past. It is true that popular pressure cannot be applied to the Soviet government which is not accountable to the people it governs. However, if the West turns its back on the Soviet Union, progress will be impossible. It would be wrong to lay the blame for the arms race entirely at the door of one or other of the superpowers. Both have been responsible. Both have used military power to pursue their interests. We should remember that, although the West has good reason to fear the military strength and intentions of the Russians, they too have good reason to fear us. There is no alternative but for the two superpowers to try to reach agreement.

Disarmament would involve a lengthy process of stage-by-stage reductions. Neither side would suddenly be defenceless. Both superpowers would be committed to binding agreements; each of which would have to be fulfilled before the next steps were taken. But once such a process began it would become easier to resolve the difficult problem of which weapons to include, and what is meant by 'equal reductions'. The actual process of talking and of reaching agreement on some issues might lead to a more trusting relationship between the superpowers which could help to resolve some of the basic political conflicts between East and West which underpin the arms race. Both processes would have to continue hand-in-hand if significant disarmament was to be achieved.

The key question, however, is how should these negotiations be organised? Should they be left to the quiet 'behind closed doors' diplomacy of superpowers or should they be under the control and gaze of the United Nations? Should the aim be to reach small and fairly straightforward 'partial' agreements on particular weapons or issues, or should there be a grand 'comprehensive programme' of disarmament with clearly worked out stages? There are many ideas about how such talks might proceed. But once they are under way it would be easier to tackle several other aspects of the arms race.

The European theatre is one part of the world where the superpowers' military forces are face-to-face and therefore an area of considerable tension. Several suggestions have been put forward for reducing this. Some people have suggested that efforts be made to eliminate battlefield nuclear weapons on both sides. Attempts have also been made to try to reduce the conventional forces of both alliances in Europe, but with little success. This is a crucial area since NATO European governments will not be prepared to place less reliance on nuclear weapons while they perceive the Warsaw Pact to have such a lead in conventional forces. But the talks on these issues were so difficult that the two sides were still unable, in 1986, even to agree how many soldiers each side had in Europe! In 1982 talks began between the Russians and Americans in Geneva about possible reductions in theatre nuclear weapons. These finally led to the signing of the INF Treaty in 1987.

United Nations headquarters in New York

One of the central tasks of the UN is to promote peace. Yet increasingly the superpowers and others have by-passed it in their arms control negotiations.

BRITAIN AND THE BOMB — BAN THE BOMB !

1 As the number and sophistication of nuclear weapons increases, the chances of a nuclear war become greater. Britain's weapons contribute towards this danger. Unilateral disarmament would stop at least a part of this deadly arms race and would signal to the rest of the world the dangers of abandoning nuclear weapons were less than keeping them. It could also be an important first step to world-wide nuclear disarmament.

2 Because Britain has a great concentration of nuclear weapons and command facilities on its territory, this makes it a primary target in any nuclear war, whether or not Britain uses its nuclear weapons first. This puts Britain's entire civilian population in great peril.

3 How could Britain ever take on the might of Russian nuclear forces on her own? If the Russians launched a small-scale attack on Britain to which Britain replied with its *Polaris* missiles, that would only result in massive Soviet retaliation which would completely destroy the country. Polaris missiles could only really be used after a massive attack on Britain. But, would there be any point if we were all dead? The British nuclear deterrent is, in fact, unusable except in a war in which the Americans were also using nuclear weapons. But in that case we wouldn't need it. So we don't need a nuclear deterrent.

4 What could be gained from fighting a nuclear war? If millions died what would they have died for? All that would be left after a nuclear war would be a radio-active, poisonous wasteland ruled by the police and army, forcing the surviving population to try to put the pieces together again.

5 Would Britain be defenceless without nuclear weapons? Sweden, Norway, Denmark, Austria, Switzerland and indeed most countries in the world seem to feel safe without having nuclear weapons. Canada got rid of US nuclear weapons on its territory in 1978 and no-one has attacked yet. It is still a member of NATO. Britain could put up a strong defence against the Russians using modern conventional forces.

6 Britain can't afford to wait for multilateral disarmament. The dangers are too great. Governments have usually used multilateral talks as an excuse to increase their weapons levels while pretending to discuss reductions. How can we pin all our faith on hopes that multilateral talks will be successful when, despite multilateral negotiations, the numbers of nuclear weapons grew from 3 in 1945 to well over 50 000 in the early 1980s?

7 Some people say that NATO would be seriously weakened if Britain abandoned its nuclear weapons. Britain's forces account for only 2 per cent of NATO nuclear forces. No-one would miss them if they went; the Americans have never said they needed them anyway. In any case each side has such a massive 'overkill' that the very idea of a nuclear balance is meaningless. Britain's dropping out would hardly affect NATO nuclear strength.

8 The threat to use nuclear weapons is morally wrong. Any defence based upon the threat to kill millions of innocent men, women and children is repugnant and ought to be rejected. It is impossible to provide lasting peace and security for the world by the threat to destroy it.

9 If the Americans get themselves involved in a war with the Russians, then many American nuclear weapons in Britain would be a high priority target for nuclear attack. Only by getting rid of nuclear weapons completely could Britain reduce that danger.

10 Of course, any decision to disarm unilaterally would involve risks. No-one can be absolutely certain that Britain would be totally safe from nuclear attack. But it isn't now! Surely the risks involved in disarmament are nothing compared with those Britain is running at the moment? Opponents say that if nuclear weapons are abandoned war will be made more likely; Nuclear disarmers say that war is certain if we don't!

BRITAIN AND THE BOMB — KEEP THE BOMB !

1 Nuclear weapons have helped to keep the peace since the end of the Second World War. Britain does not have to fear that the Russians might use their overwhelming conventional superiority against it. Nuclear weapons have proved to be a cheap and very effective deterrent. If Britain relied just on conventional weapons its defences would be less effective and very much more expensive.

2 Although Europe's defence relies on the guarantee of US support, Britain's nuclear deterrent is an extra insurance. The Russians might gamble that the USA would not go to war for the sake of Britain, but they would not doubt the willingness of the British to defend themselves. Their nuclear weapons could wreak such damage on the Soviet Union that no sane Soviet leader would ever risk an attack on Britain. It would not be worth it.

3 The nuclear disarmers are right to point out the horrors of nuclear war, but wrong to argue that they can be avoided by unilateral disarmament. An effective nuclear deterrent *can* achieve it though. The horrors of a nuclear war cannot be avoided by turning away and hoping that Britain will never be attacked, but by deterring such an attack through the threat of retaliation. That is the only defence against nuclear attack.

4 Nuclear disarmers apparently believe that if Britain abandoned its nuclear weapons the Russians would never use them against it. This is a stupid view. Britain is bound to be involved in any European war because of its position for American reinforcements and its value as a base. It would be a prime target whether or not it was neutral. Why risk a fleet of bombers and pilots to knock out Portsmouth when a one-megaton warhead would do just as well? Deterrence is the only certain way of preventing a nuclear war.

5 If Britain did pull out of NATO, that would seriously weaken the alliance. It would encourage the Soviet Union to try to destroy that challenge to its power and influence while NATO was in a weak position. If Britain got rid of its nuclear weapons and left NATO it would make war *more* not *less* likely.

6 Is conventional warfare more acceptable than nuclear war? As far as Britain is concerned, a conventional war could be almost as destructive as a nuclear one (though without the radiation side-effects). Even in the Second World War, conventional firebombs on Tokyo and Dresden caused more damage and killed more people than the atom bombs dropped on Hiroshima and Nagasaki.

7 The Americans are sometimes described as Britain's real enemy. Nothing is further from the truth. It is only through American support that Europe has been able to stand up to the superior military might of the Soviet Union. They have put their nuclear weapons at Britain's disposal and risked the lives of US servicemen in the defence of Europe. Britain must play its part by contributing towards that defence. Britain's nuclear weapons and the facilities for the US forces are part of its contribution.

8 Unilateral disarmament would be a complete leap in the dark from which Britain would gain nothing. If Britain holds out until *all* sides are ready to negotiate disarmament it could, as a nuclear power, have a lot of influence on the talks. If it unilaterally abandons its weapons it gives away all its bargaining chips for nothing. No-one would follow its example. The result would simply be that Britain would be less secure in a world where other countries maintain a strong defence.

One idea that received widespread support was the plan to make Europe a nuclear-free zone in which nuclear weapons would be eliminated from the entire region and all the nuclear weapons states would agree not to use nuclear weapons against free-zone countries. A European nuclear-free zone is an attractive idea because, by removing nuclear forces from European territory it would eliminate many of the fears and risks of nuclear conflict in Europe. But there are several problems involved. Europe has two fully-fledged nuclear weapons states, Britain and France, who might be reluctant to lose their special status. There is also the question of whether Europe would still want to rely on the American nuclear 'umbrella' as a last resort to deter Soviet aggression, and whether the Americans would still be willing to come to Europe's aid if nuclear weapons were removed from Europe. Finally, it would remain true that nuclear missiles based in the Soviet Union could hit targets in Europe. In the end it comes down to a balance of risks: would a nuclear-free Europe be at a greater risk of nuclear attack or of Warsaw Pact invasion than it is now?

Some people argue that the dangers of nuclear war in Europe can be reduced if greater reliance is put upon conventional weapons and if money is spent upon building up conventional forces. It can be argued that the building-up of force is clearly a continuation of the arms race. One approach, however, overcomes this criticism by linking conventional defence to nuclear disarmament. It is argued that if European nations were to abandon their nuclear weapons and rely instead on an alternative defence made up of defensive weapons using the latest technology, they could reduce the risks of nuclear attack, yet be able to deter aggression against them. Such alternative defences might involve the deployment of increased numbers of precision-guided weapons against attacking land or sea forces. It could involve the creation of citizen armies trained in combat to harass an invader. It could involve the development of a programme of nuclear shelters for the civilian population. The supporters of this view argue that it makes it possible for countries to turn away from reliance on nuclear weapons which is becoming more and more dangerous and to a more flexible and realistic way of deterring aggression. It could be achieved without waiting for lengthy multilateral negotiations. But most importantly, it could reverse the arms race by concentrating on defence in a way that could not be seen as a threat to the other side. There would, it is argued, be no need for the other side to go on building up its forces to defend itself against possible aggression. If the link which forces each side to step up its armaments to match the other could be broken, then, say the supporters of alternative defence, within a short space of time it would be possible to make significant reductions in overall spending on weapons.

Possible strategies

Some proposals, whether or not linked to ideas of alternative defence, call upon Britain and France to renounce their possession of nuclear weapons unilaterally as a bold and direct step to reverse the arms race and reduce the chances of nuclear conflict in Europe. The detailed arguments for and against have already been considered in this chapter, but unilateral nuclear disarmament may be the quickest and most effective way of demonstrating that nuclear disarmament is possible. It may therefore be the best way of accelerating the slow complex process of disarmament. But, if linked to increases in conventional forces, such disarmament would not necessarily save any money for use in other areas. Although during the 1980s there was growing support within Britain for the idea of unilateral disarmament, a majority of the population favoured retaining the independent nuclear deterrent. The French did not show the slighest interest in such ideas; they were determined to remain a nuclear state.

Even a partial success in achieving nuclear disarmament in Europe may make success elsewhere in the world more likely. It may make it easier to propose nuclear-free zones in other areas of tension such as the Middle East, southern Africa and South East Asia. And if the nuclear arsenals of the superpowers are being reduced this might reduce the temptation and justification for Third World nations to try to develop their own nuclear weapons.

Anti-nuclear moves in the South Pacific

The Pacific Ocean is another area in which the superpowers carry on their armed rivalry. In the north, the Soviet Union has both nuclear and conventional military forces poised for action against China, Taiwan and Japan, and also against the large naval forces of the USA, many of which are armed with nuclear weapons. The USA also has many military bases in the region, some of which store nuclear weapons.

There has been growing opposition to nuclear weapons during the 1980s in the South Pacific region. Although there are no nuclear weapon states and no nuclear bases in that region, there has been a growing determination to limit the superpower competition and prevent the nations of the South Pacific being dragged into the conflict. The Australian government refused to help in flight testing the MX missile for the Americans. The New Zealand government withdrew the rights of the US navy to come into its ports unless they guaranteed that there were no nuclear weapons aboard. The Americans refused to do this. The New Zealand policy provoked considerable tension between the two countries. There is also fierce opposition in the region to France's use of the Mururoa Atoll to test its nuclear warheads. The local people resent French misuse of the territory and the potential danger of radioactive pollution that the tests may cause.

In August 1985 the South Pacific became the second populated region, after Latin America, to establish a nuclear weapon-free zone. The treaty bans the presence of nuclear weapons, or their manufacturing or testing, anywhere within the territory of the South Pacific states, up to their nineteen-kilometre sea limits. One important exception to this ban is that the treaty does not seek to prevent visiting ships or aircraft from carrying nuclear weapons; but it does prevent their being permanently stationed in the area. The nuclear weapons states have been invited to sign the treaty on behalf of the islands they control in the area. This provides a serious problem for France, because, if it signed it would have to stop its nuclear tests in the South Pacific.

International co-operation

Nuclear weapons must be the first priority for disarmament
because of the threat they pose to life on this planet. But we should
remember that, out of every $10 that is spent on armaments, $8
goes on conventional forces, so considerable effort will have to be
spent on reducing conventional armaments if the arms race is to be
reversed. It is hard to see how substantial conventional disarmament
could ever be achieved, as long as nations ultimately rely on force to
solve their problems. Perhaps it is unrealistic to expect such things to
change, but some clear steps could be taken to improve the chances
of solving disputes and conflicts without resort to armed force
between nations. This would require much greater influence and
power being given to an organisation like the United Nations which
is at the moment quite weak. It would have to oversee and organise
international efforts to solve major world problems such as the
distribution of wealth and the use of resources. It could, for example,
levy taxes on the rich nations and redistribute the funds to the
poorer ones. It might oversee a fair sharing of the world's resources
of minerals and fossil fuels, and it might even organise tight controls
over nuclear power generation and nuclear fuels. But these kinds of
things could only ever be achieved by a revolution in the way
nations behave. The governments of nations would have to accept
the same kinds of control on *their* behaviour as those they impose on
their own citizens.

Perhaps the ideas of 'world government' are too idealistic and
impractical. There are however, other avenues of progress.
International agreements could be reached, without forcing countries
to submit themselves to the authority of an international body like
the United Nations. Certain kinds of weapons, particularly those
which are indiscriminate in their effects and which cause exceptional
suffering (such as tumbling bullets, napalm and cluster bombs) could
be prohibited. Restrictions could be placed on the arms trade.
There is an urgent need, for example, to ban the production and use
of chemical weapons. There is the danger of a renewed arms race in
chemical weapons in view of US plans to modernise its stockpile, and
because of the increasing use of chemical weapons by Iraq in the
Middle East. Several Western companies have made it easy for Iraq
to make chemical weapons by selling the necessary constituents.

Trade with troubled parts of world or with governments who
abuse human rights could be banned. But here too, national self-
interest would have to give way to a sense of a greater good. As the
US government found when it placed restrictions on the arms it
exported in the late 1970s, it is no good one country cutting down if
other arms exporters (like the French and Israelis) simply fill the gap.
So even here widespread international agreement would be needed.
Moreover, as we have seen, arms exports are a major means of
making arms industries profitable for countries. Therefore a
reduction in the arms trade and progress in conventional
disarmament would reinforce one another.

Nations will, no doubt, still try to make or buy arms to fight their
battles as long as there are disputes which cannot be solved in any
other way. Perhaps we will have to learn to live with the fact that
there will always be conflict and war in a world of competing
nations, religions and beliefs, divided into haves and have-nots. But
that does not mean that there is no point in trying to develop
effective ways of helping nations to resolve conflicts peacefully. It
may be argued that such hopes are too idealistic and that nations

will continue to look after their own interests and build up the necessary armaments to do so. While few would deny the right of nations to defend themselves against aggression, it is clear, as this book has pointed out, that the arms race does not, in the end, increase the security of nations, but rather reduces it. For all the armaments at their disposal, do the British, the Russians or the Americans feel safer today than they did twenty years ago? The arms race involves the world's nations in huge risks and diverts resources away from programmes that could help to create a safer and happier world.

The road to disarmament will not be a clear and easy one to follow. But several paths have been discussed in this chapter which open up real possibilities of achieving a safer and more secure foundation for peace in the world. Perhaps it may not be possible to do away with nuclear weapons altogether: it may simply be impossible to 'disinvent' something. To call for the elimination of nuclear weapons is in some ways like trying to ban drugs. Who could be sure that someone, somewhere, does not have any? Another problem is that, as with drugs, a lot of people really do want to keep them, because they feel they need them, or because they make a living from them.

We may only be able to reduce the nuclear stockpiles to the levels of the 1950s, when a few hundred nuclear warheads were regarded as an adequate deterrent. In those circumstances an anti-missile defensive shield on both sides might make some sense. But surely the goal should be to strive to do away completely with these weapons which threaten the very existence of life on this planet? But to do this, the world's nuclear states will have to be persuaded that their security will be greater without such weapons than with them.

Any solution to the problem of nuclear weapons is closely tied to conventional strengths too. We cannot deal with one without tackling the other, because they are both means which countries have adopted to defend themselves and to win conflicts. So it follows that we must try to tackle the basic conflicts which divide nations from one another. No-one should underestimate the enormity of such a task. But that is not an argument against at least making a start. And efforts to reduce the stockpile of nuclear weapons is a good place to begin.

In a very real sense we have no alternative but to tread this path because in no other way can the security of all nations be ensured. A firm and stable foundation for world peace cannot be built upon the constant threat to destroy civilisation and millions of innocent people. Nobody seriously suggests either superpower wants to start a nuclear war, or really believes that it can win one, but we have reached a stage where the weapons we have created to defend us pose a greater threat to peace than the problems they were designed to meet. We *can* tread a different path. The arms race is a product of human decisions. Those decisions can be reversed and we must all play a part in ensuring that they are.

9 Further resources on the arms race

Introductory books

An issue to debate: the nuclear question, Tressel Publications, 1982
> *Good material which is aimed to get students questioning and thinking*

Barrow, S. and Webster, S, *Who makes a killing? Britain and the international arms trade*, CAAT, 1987
> *Sets out clearly the facts about the arms trade and Britain's role in it*

Briggs, R, *When the wind blows*, Hamish Hamilton, 1982
> *Well-known cartoon book on what can happen to ordinary people in a nuclear war*

Cox, J, *Overkill*, Penguin, 1981
> *Survey of weapons and short history of the arms race*

Kidron, M. and Smith, D, *The War Atlas*, Pluto Press, 1983
> *The arms race facts and figures in map form; colourful, fascinating and accurate*

Litherland, A, *A short guide to disarmament*, Housmans, 1982
> *A short book. Sets out ways of disarming and some of the obstacles; gives details of treaties*

Richardson, R. *Learning for change in world society*. World Studies Project, 1976
> *Excellent fund of ideas for experiential approaches to teaching about conflict*

More advanced books

Alternative Defence Commission, *Without the bomb*, Paladin
> *Sets out possible non-nuclear defence policies for Britain*

Barnaby, F, *What on earth is Star Wars?* Fourth Estate Ltd., 1986
> *Explains what it is, what it is supposed to do, and gives arguments for and against. Clear and readable*

Freedman, L. *Atlas of global strategy*, Macmillan, 1985
> *More than an atlas: outlines the main features of conflict since 1945. Lots of case studies and helpful graphs. Helps to make sense of complex issues*

Goodwin, P, *Nuclear war: the facts on our survival*, Macmillan, 1982
> *Very thorough, clear and well illustrated*

Greene, O, *London after the bomb*, OUP, 1982
> *It could be any city; a grim but accurate account of the destruction caused by a nuclear attack*

Harris, R. and Paxman, J. *A higher form of killing*, Granada, 1983
> *History of gas and germ warfare since 1914*

Hayes, P. and Zarksy, L, *American Lake: nuclear peril in the Pacific*, Penguin, 1987
> *Describes the superpower conflict and militarisation of the Pacific*

Neild, R, *How to make up your mind about the bomb*, Andre Deutsch, 1981
> *Needs careful reading, but does help to make the arguments clear*

Prins, G, *Defended to death*, Penguin, 1983
> *Detailed (but not easy) book about changing nuclear strategy, the military-industrial complex, the case against nuclear defence of Europe and alternatives to it*

Suddaby, A, *The nuclear war game*, Longman, 1983. (Also available in seven separate booklets under the title, *Nuclear weapons and warfare*.)
> *Thorough, detailed and accurate; covers the effects, arms race and strategies. Good for reference but no index*

Townsend, P, *The Postman of Nagasaki*, Penguin
> *True, harrowing account of a survivor of the bombing*

Turner, J. and SIPRI, *Arms in the '80s*, Taylor & Francis, 1985
> *A summary of key developments in the arms race in the mid 1980s*

Facts and figures

It is very difficult to get hold of reliable figures which make sense; you will find that different sources give different figures for, eg. the numbers of weapons held by the Soviet Union and Warsaw Pact. However, the following are good sources:

General arms race issues: Kidron, M. and Smith, D, *The War Atlas*, Pluto Press

Types of nuclear weapons: Rogers, P, *Guide to nuclear weapons*. Bradford School of Peace Studies. Available from Housmans Bookshop, 5 Caledonian Road, London N1 (latest edition 1987)

Military forces of the world compared: International Institute for Strategic Studies, *The military balance*. Updated annually; very detailed; includes information on nuclear and conventional weapons, numbers and types

The effects of nuclear weapons/civil defence: Clarke, R, *London under attack*, Basil Blackwell, 1986. Very well researched. Detailed figures on London, but could be any city. Considers Britain as a whole and covers environmental effects such as nuclear winter

Military spending and the social costs: World Priorities Inc, *World military and social expenditures*. Published annually; gives figures on war casualties, spending on armaments compared with spending on health and welfare etc. Clear and compelling statistics. Excellent reference material. Good value for money. Available from ADIU, Mantell Building, University of Sussex, Flamer, Brighton, Sussex, BN1 9RF

Organisations providing information

If you write to these organisations it helps if you say exactly what you need. Also, since they usually survive on small budgets, enclose at least a stamped addressed envelope.

Australian Peace Committee
Box 32, Trades Hall, Goulburn Street, Sydney, NSW 2000

British Atlantic Committee
30a St James' Square, London SW1
  Provides resources and speakers on nuclear issues; pro NATO

Campaign Against Arms Trade (CAAT)
11 Goodwin Street, London N4 3HQ
  Aims to end British involvement in the arms trade

Campaign for Nuclear Disarmament (CND)
22–24 Underwood Street, London N1 7JG
  Wants Britain to renounce nuclear weapons as a first step towards world disarmament

Center for Defense Information
303 Capitol Gallery W, 600 Maryland Avenue SW, Washington DC, 20024

Coalition for Peace through Security
27–31 Whitehall, London SW1A 2BX
  Believes in strong defences

European Nuclear Disarmament (END)
11 Goodwin Street, London N4 3HQ
  Works for a nuclear-free Europe

Friends of the Earth
377 City Road, London EC1V 1NA
  Concerned with the environment, including the effects of nuclear energy

Greenpeace (Australia)
155 Pirie Street, Adelaide 5000

Greenpeace (UK)
36 Graham St. London N1
  Opposes destruction of the natural environment; includes opposition to French tests

National Peace Council
29 Great James Street, London WC1H 3ES
  A link organisation for different peace groups

National Peace Institute Foundation
110 Maryland Avenue NE, Washington DC, 20002

Nuclear-Free & Independent Pacific Coordinating Committee
PO Box A243, Sydney South, NSW 2000

Peace Pledge Union
6 Endsleigh Street, London WC1H ODX
  Pacifist; against all forms of militarism

Peace Tax Campaign
1a Hollybush Place, London E2 9QX
  Encourages people to withold taxes that pay for armaments

United Kingdom Atomic Energy Authority
Information Services Branch, 11 Charles II St, London SW1Y 4QP
  Provides information on nuclear power

United Nations Association (UNA)
3 Whitehall Court, London SW1A 2EL
  To support the peace work of the United Nations and to persuade the British government to live up to the principles of the UN Charter

World Disarmament Campaign (WDC)
45–47 Blythe Street, London 32 6LX
  To promote the ideas of general and complete disarmament as set out by the UN

United Nations Association Disarmament & Peace Committee
28 Elizabeth Street, Melbourne, Victoria 3000

United Nations Non Governmental Organisations Committee on Disarmament
777 UN Plaza, New York, NY 10017

US Peace Council
7E 15th Street, Room 408, New York, NY 10003

Official sources of information

Government departments provide leaflets and booklets and will give information to members of the public on specific issues.

Defence policy: The Ministry of Defence, Main Building, Whitehall, London SW1 2HB. A film, commissioned by the Ministry of Defence, called *The Peace Game* (colour, 28 mins, 1982) is available from the Central Film Library

Civil defence: The Home Office, 50 Queen Anne's Gate, London SW1. The Home Office have published a few leaflets and booklets on civil defence. These include *Protect and Survive*, 1980, (out of print: try public libraries) and *Domestic Nuclear Shelters*, 1981, (available from HMSO)

Arms control and disarmament policy: Foreign and Commonwealth Office, Downing Street (East), London, SW1A 2AH. Provide a number of booklets on deterrence and government disarmament policies

Independent sources of information

Reliable technical information can be obtained from the Armament and Disarmament Information Unit (ADIU) at Science Policy Research Unit, University of Sussex, Brighton, BN1 9RF

The Stockholm International Peace Research Institute (SIPRI) also has an information department. The address is SIPRI, Pipers vag 28, S-171 73 Solna, Sweden

Only contact these organisations with detailed enquiries if you can't find the answers from other sources.

Tape/slide sets

A better road to peace, Central Film Library.
Gerrards Cross, London SL9 8TN. (Also in Film & video formats)

  Puts the argument for Britain's nuclear deterrent and role in NATO

Former, B, *Nuclear weapons*, Mary Glasgow Publications Ltd, Kineton, Warwick, CV35 OBR
  Detailed filmstrip on history, strategies and arguments. Accurate but fairly advanced level

Suddaby, A, *The threat of nuclear war,*
Focal Point Ltd, Portsmouth, PO1 2BR
  Thirty slides with notes on the arms race and disarmament. Visually excellent and accurate. For older students

Films and videos

All of the titles listed below can be obtained from Concord Films Council Ltd, 201 Felixstowe Road, Ipswich, Suffolk, IP3 9BJ. Films are 16 mm and videos are available in VHS, Betamax and U-Matic formats. Videos are generally cheaper to hire and definitely cheaper to send.

F = film version; V = video version; all listed films are in colour.

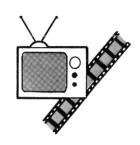

A change in the weather	Discussion of the global effects of nuclear winter	V	25 mins	1984
A guide to Armageddon	Excellent, devastating account of what a 1MT bomb would do to a city like London	FV	28 mins	1982
Atomic cafe	Uses only US propaganda and military film to show American attitudes to the bomb from the '40s to the '60s. Excellent material	F	89 mins	1982
Attention	Superb cartoon about weapons technology	F	12 mins	1959
The Bomb	Jonathan Dimbleby's chilling analysis of recent trends in the arms race. Excellent film	FV	70 mins	1980
Commonsense: Greenham Actions 1982	Dramatic account of the actions of the women at the Greenham Common Airforce base against cruise missile deployment	V	40 mins	1983
John Hersey's Hiroshima	Schools programme about Hiroshima. Excerpts from the book plus newsreel	V	20 mins	1980
The multinationals: the only difference between the men and the boys is the size of their toys	Detailed account of the world of the arms manufacturers and traders	V	50 mins	1982
The need to know	Civil defence: shows how inadequate local medical resources would be after a nuclear explosion	V	40 mins	1983
Nixon's secret legacy	Life for those whose fingers are on the button in a US Minuteman missile silo	FV	30 mins	1975
Nuclear free Europe	Former NATO military men explain the risks of reliance on nuclear weapons to defend Europe	V	24 mins	1983
Picadon	The bombing of Hiroshima. Horrific scenes	F	8 mins	
The shape of wars to come	How 'Star Wars' could become a reality	FV	27 mins	1981
Video from Russia: the people speak	American TV team interview ordinary Russians in the street about jobs, lives and hopes	V	58 mins	1985
War: notes on nuclear war	Traces the development of the nuclear arms race from Hiroshima to the present	FV	58 mins	1983
Weapons in space	The history and future of Star Wars	V	30 mins	1984
We've always done it this way	Account of Lucas workers' alternatives to defence production	FV	50 mins	1978

Index